The
INSTRUCTIONAL
LEADER and
the Brain

This book is written in loving memory of my beautiful sister, Mary Frances Merwin—une directrice très extraordinaire—whose spirit lives in the many she loved, taught, and inspired.

The
INSTRUCTIONAL LEADER and
the Brain

Using Neuroscience to Inform Practice

Margaret Glick

Foreword by **Pat Wolfe**

CORWIN
A SAGE Company

CORWIN
A SAGE Company

FOR INFORMATION:

Corwin

A SAGE Company

2455 Teller Road

Thousand Oaks, California 91320

(800) 233-9936

Fax: (800) 417-2466

www.corwin.com

SAGE Ltd.

1 Oliver's Yard

55 City Road

London EC1Y 1SP

United Kingdom

SAGE India Pvt. Ltd.

B 1/I 1 Mohan Cooperative Industrial Area

Mathura Road, New Delhi 110 044

India

SAGE Asia-Pacific Pte. Ltd.

33 Pekin Street #02-01

Far East Square

Singapore 048763

Acquisitions Editor: Arnis Burvikovs

Associate Editor: Desirée A. Bartlett

Editorial Assistant: Kimberly Greenberg

Production Editor: Amy Schroller

Copy Editor: Tina Hardy

Typesetter: C&M Digitals (P) Ltd.

Proofreader: Rae-Ann Goodwin

Indexer: Beth Nauman-Montana

Cover Designer: Karine Hovsepian

Permissions Editor: Karen Ehrmann

Copyright © 2011 by Corwin

Illustrations created by Min Sung Ku.

Printed in the United States of America

Library of Congress Cataloging-in-Publication Data

Glick, Margaret.

The instructional leader and the brain : using neuroscience to inform practice / Margaret Glick; foreword by Pat Wolfe.

p. cm.
Includes bibliographical references and index.

ISBN 978-1-4129-8822-3 (pbk.)

1. Learning, Psychology of. 2. Learning—Physiological aspects. 3. Neurosciences. I. Title.

LB1060.G558 2011
370.15′23—dc23   2011024512

This book is printed on acid-free paper.

11 12 13 14 15 10 9 8 7 6 5 4 3 2 1

Contents

Foreword

Pat Wolfe

It was in the early 1990s that I became interested in the applications of neuroscience (brain research) to educational practice. After all, since teachers are teaching brains, doesn't it make sense to understand as much as possible about how they learn? Perhaps we would find some answers to the most vexing problems teacher face, such as why some children have difficulty learning to read or how to get students to pay attention in class. As I began to read and talk to neuroscientists, I also began to incorporate what I was learning into my workshops and seminars. These workshops on the applications of brain research to educational practice found an enthusiastic audience of educators at every level from preschool through the university. Educators were fascinated with the research and the implications for their classrooms. I was not the only educator working in this new field; Renate and Jeff Caine, Eric Jensen, David Sousa, and Bob Sylwester also shared interest in this new field.

The popularity of the workshops began to present a problem; none of us had the time to honor all the requests. To meet the need of more presenters, I developed a training-of-trainers program. I selected educators (teachers, administrators, staff developers, school psychologists) who were considered tops in their field and offered to train them to conduct workshops and seminars in their own schools and districts.

Over the past 15 years, nearly 500 educators have taken advantage of these training-of-trainers sessions. Among the first to attend was an excellent teacher named Margaret Glick. She was a natural, very successful teacher, and she immediately began incorporating the research and brain-compatible strategies in her own classroom. When she moved into administration as a coach, principal, and superintendent, she carried her expertise with her and expanded the applications of the research to curriculum, assessment, and leadership. Later, the university classes she taught on brain development and cognition were favorites of new and experienced teachers.

Many years ago, Dr. Bruce Joyce developed a classification of teachers related to their staff development experiences. At the highest level he described the "omnivores," those who not only sought out professional development workshops and seminars but immediately incorporated what they learned into their work. Glick certainly fits this category, having participated in a wide range of training in coaching, differentiated instruction, working with students of poverty, assessment, guided language acquisition, standards, math, and thinking maps, among others.

Perhaps the most important contribution Glick makes is the rationale for why leaders of schools need to understand current findings from neuroscience. This book provides a framework for instructional leaders to use the ideas and research on the brain in their unique roles as evaluators, communicators, and professional developers.

Glick's wide range of successful experience at all levels of education has served her well. She practices what she preaches. The book draws on the elements of effective brain-compatible instruction and clear, precise presentation of the research; opportunities to practice recall; and strategies for application of the research at the leadership level.

Anyone in a leadership capacity will benefit from the information provided in this book. Here is an opportunity to understand and engage in the brain-compatible activities of a true instructional leader.

Preface

BRAIN-COMPATIBLE INSTRUCTIONAL LEADERSHIP

A shift occurred in the 1980s when a body of research found that principals of effective schools were instructional leaders (Brookover & Lezotte, 1982). Since then, evidence of the importance of instructional leadership at schools continues to mount. The role of principal has shifted from that of manager-administrator to instructional leader. How might we define an instructional leader? There are critical skills and knowledge that set an instructional leader apart from a manager-administrator.

Instructional leaders who understand how people learn hold the potential to be game-changers. They can better recognize effective methods, communicate and calibrate what effective learning looks and sounds like to others, and finally, support teachers in their continuing professional growth (Elmore, City, Fiarman, & Teitel, 2009; Fullan, 2001; Reeves, 2006).

Some of the roles inherent to an instructional leader include resource provider, instructional resource, good communicator, and visible presence in the classroom (Whitaker, 1997). Some of the skills required of an instructional leader include interpersonal, research and evaluation, planning, and observational (Phillips, 2002). Taken together, these roles and skills help to transform a school leader into an instructional and learning leader.

Imagine an instructional leader that is an expert in how people learn. How might that impact a school? First, the instructional leader would be comfortable and confident with one of the most important tasks of an instructional leader, the task of observing teaching and learning in the classroom. In the event the observation is occurring with colleagues, the level of competence and confidence that an instructional leader possesses may add a beneficial spark that leads to creative problem solving and adaptive action, as opposed to hand-wringing. This level of comfort and confidence probably means that teachers and students become accustomed to the principal stopping by, unannounced, to get a glimpse of what and how students are learning on any given day and to keep his or her finger on the pulse of the learning going on in classrooms. Instructional leaders that understand how people learn are leaders who can use their own guiding principles as a compass, instead of having to rely forever on a checklist of strategies from a publisher far, far away. These instructional leaders are able to take what is happening in the classroom and find the next level of work required in order to continuously improve. They are able to record meaningful information from classroom visits that can act as springboards for future conversations that can make a difference (Elmore et al., 2009; Marshall, 2009). Because they understand how people learn, they understand how to give feedback in a productive and effective way, and they understand where teachers are on the continuum to become masterful instructors, therefore, the path to improvement is lit.

To understand how people learn, we must examine and develop understandings and become comfortable with the learning organ. We must come to understand the brain. That black box is the originator of thought, of responses, of learning. And in education, learning is what it's all about.

WHY THIS BOOK? WHY NOW?

Instructional leaders need resources that speak to the most important and high leverage issue at hand—student learning. This book provides the information to incorporate the knowledge, skills, and steps to becoming a masterful instructional leader at a school site. By marrying the fields of cognitive science, neuroscience, educational leadership, and instruction, this book provides a cohesive framework to understand how the brain learns and how an instructional leader can use this information to improve student achievement.

Never before have educators been charged with such a complex and worthy task of leaving no child behind with regard to educational progress. Complex challenges call for thoughtful solutions. No checklist or publisher-made form is going to provide the kind of information and data an instructional leader needs to serve as solutions for our unique contexts. Becoming learned about what we are all here for, which is learning, will serve as a solution.

What Makes This Book Unique?

This book provides a framework for understanding five elements that play crucial roles in how we learn. These five elements are as follows: (a) the impact of emotions on learning, (b) memory systems at work, (c) attention and engagement, (d) the power of processing, and (e) feedback for learning. Instructional leaders will discover things, such as why people remember some kinds of information better than others and how and why the emotional environment in a classroom can make or break critical thinking. This book breaks down ways people learn as seen through the eyes of an instructional leader. Using contexts that are familiar to educators, readers will broaden their understanding of critical features of lessons, activities, and classroom management. The book provides processes and protocols for instructional leaders to share their understanding of how the brain learns with teachers and other colleagues.

Organization of the Book

There are six chapters in the book. The first chapter acts as a brain primer, orienting the reader to structures, functions, and vocabulary of neuroscience. The next five chapters each explain a learning principle in detail and apply it to a classroom and staffroom setting. This is done through vignettes and educational scenarios. Each chapter begins by tapping the readers' prior knowledge about the topic and then relating it through stories and analogies. The neuroscience behind each principle is examined next, using unambiguous language and real-world examples that exemplify the principle. This enables instructional leaders to begin to make connections and integrate the new information with their current mental model. Overt links are made throughout each chapter with regard to how this information fits into the instructional leader's toolkit. Each chapter contains resources for the instructional leader to use with teachers. Rubrics, checklists, charts, and tables provided will allow instructional leaders avenues to incorporate new understandings in the classroom and staffroom. Each chapter provides a section linking the learning principle to the knowledge and skills of an effective instructional leader. Each chapter also provides formative assessment questions to allow readers to measure progress in their learning. Questions that might be used in a study group to extend readers' thinking with regard to each principle close each chapter.

This book will equip the instructional leader to develop necessary knowledge and skills to understand how our brains learn and recall information and what kinds of things teachers can do to encourage and elicit powerful learning and recall. The reader will learn how to spot effective instruction and student engagement in classrooms that are compatible with how the brain learns, as well as instruction that may run counter to what we know is brain compatible. Materials will be provided for the instructional leader that will assist in recording and measuring effective instruction as well as communicating with and supporting teachers who are struggling with instruction.

This book was written with the instructional leader in mind. Now, more than ever, our leaders need to understand not only what constitutes best instructional practices in the classroom but how to filter the effective from the ineffective, the mediocre from the superior, the good from the bad, and the bad from the ugly. My hope is that this book provides instructional leaders a solid framework for understanding how we can use principles from neuroscience to engage our colleagues, our teachers, and our students in relevant, robust learning.

Acknowledgments

I would like to thank the various educators with whom I have had the pleasure to work; your insights and stories fill my neural networks, as well as the pages of this book.

To the trailblazers, who years ago began linking neuroscience to education, I say thank you. I would like to thank Pat Wolfe, in particular, who I saw present years ago and have been a groupie ever since. Her generosity, contributions, and commitment to this work are extraordinary.

To my brothers and sisters who have always been my cheering section and safety net: Jim, Mary Fran, John, Mike, Matt, Anne, Jerry, and Patty. G—I could not have done this without your help.

To my husband, Brian, for his ever-present patience, love, and support, and my children Elizabeth and Daniel, for happily engaging in so many conversations about the brain with your mom, thank you.

Publisher's Acknowledgments

Corwin would like to thank the following individuals for taking the time to provide their editorial insight:

Rick Miller, Superintendent
Riverside Unified School District
Riverside, CA

Debra Mugge, Principal
Springbrook High School
Silver Spring, MD

Julie Prescott, Assessment
    Coordinator
Vallivue High School
Caldwell, ID

Leslie Standerfer, Principal
Estrella Foothills High School
Goodyear, AZ

Ellen Weber, Director
MITA International
    Brain-Based Center
Pittsford, NY

About the Author

Margaret Glick is an independent consultant specializing in linking neuroscience, cognitive science, and education. Her passion is promoting educators' practical understanding of current research and its implications in schools. This passion stems from the belief in educators' capacity to reach the highest level of learning and thinking in order to continuously improve their practice.

Margaret's professional background includes work as an elementary and middle school teacher, full-time mentor teacher, instructional coach, assistant principal, staff developer, principal/superintendent, and university instructor. These opportunities and experiences have brought a range of skills and understanding to her work in education. In working with a wide diversity of school districts, from the very small, rural settings, to the large, urban districts, Margaret has adapted and differentiated her methods to achieve success in varied learning communities. Her expertise includes providing professional development, coaching, and a variety of assistance to various educational groups.

CHAPTER 1

A Brain Primer— Major Structures and Their Functions

Education is discovering the brain and that's about the best news there could be . . . anyone who does not have a thorough, holistic grasp of the brain's architecture, purposes, and main ways of operating is as far behind the times as an automobile designer without a full understanding of engines.

—Leslie Hart (1983)

- *Have you ever wondered how the brain works?*
- *Have you ever wondered what the different parts of the brain do?*
- *Have you ever wondered why some see effort as futile and others see it as imperative?*

The brain is a complex organ whose relationship with learning is undeniable. The primary charge of an instructional leader is to increase learning. Analyze the learning organ and begin to understand how we learn. To develop understanding, it is critical to have anchors of information from which to build upon.

This chapter will act as that anchor. Because the remaining chapters in the book may assume knowledge of this chapter, it will serve as a foundation for greater comprehension throughout the remainder of the book. This chapter will discuss the major structures and functions of the brain, what the brain looks and feels like, and how those structures differ in their functions. Readers will explore deep inside the brain to discover the mysteries of this miraculous organ.

Does not understanding how the brain works preclude being an effective instructional leader? Probably not, especially for those who have already enjoyed years of success as an instructional leader. The truth is that brain-compatible methods have been used forever, because they work well, and some people instinctively employ these methods naturally. For those who would benefit from a more deliberate, analytical approach, this book codifies these methods, so instead of relying on experience as the only teacher, an instructional leader can enlist the help of science as well.

An unusually fitting analogy for the workings of the human brain was written by Thomas Armstrong in his book, *Neurodiversity* (2010). Instead of comparing the brain to computers or control towers, which seems to be common, he compares it to a complex ecosystem. In response to comparisons to the brain being like a machine, he writes as follows:

> It isn't characterized by levers and gears, wires and sockets, or even the simple binary codes of computers. It isn't hardware or software. It's wetware. And it's messy . . . . The body of a neuron, or brain cell, looks like an exotic tropical tree with numerous branches. The electric crackling of neuronal networks mimics heat lightning in a forest. The undulations of neurotransmitters moving between neurons resemble the ocean tides. (pp. 9–10)

Aside from the beautifully descriptive imagery of this writing, I think this analogy serves as a reminder that understanding the brain is something within everyone's reach. Although it might be complex, it is an integral part of our world and our lives. Some educators I have worked with have expressed the notion that the brain is somehow too complex to understand. They shy away from the topic in an effort to "leave it to the experts." Some might even argue that understanding how the brain works is not a good use of an educator's time. I would argue that the instructional leaders who understand how the brain works gain exponential understandings in every role and responsibility embedded in their charge. When I understand how the brain works, I better understand learning, teaching, responses, behaviors, communication, and motivation. I'd say that's a pretty good bang for the buck (see Figure 1.1).

BRAIN HEMISPHERES

The human brain weighs about 3 pounds, is about the size of a grapefruit, and is composed of two hemispheres. The consistency of a live brain inside the skull is about that of toothpaste, fresh out of a tube (but wouldn't stick like toothpaste). Taking both hands and making fists, then placing them, touching each other, knuckles

Figure 1.1 A Bird's Eye View of the Brain's Two Hemispheres

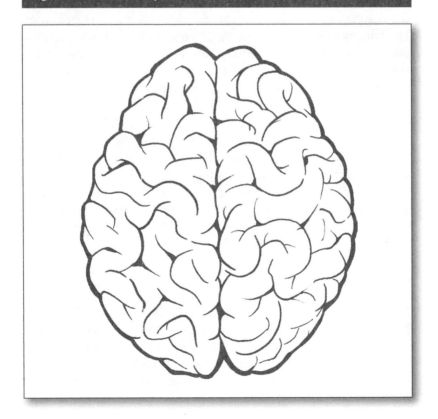

to knuckles, will create a decent model of the human brain. Like the two hands have matching elements (two index fingers, two palms, etc.), the brain's hemispheres also have matching elements. For almost every structure in one hemisphere, a matching structure in its twin exists. The right hemisphere controls the left side of your body, while the left hemisphere controls the right side. Although these hemispheres are similar in structure, there are a few differences in general function. The hemispheres of the brain excel at different kinds of thinking, which provides the benefit of various ways of sensing and perceiving. The right hemisphere tends to excel at nonverbal, spatial tasks; it helps with things like awareness, sociability, intuition, holistic thinking, estimation, intonation of speech, and visual memories, among other things. The left hemisphere excels in language and verbal and logical tasks, including things like writing and speaking, calculating, analyzing, tending to grammar and literal meaning of speech, and thinking linearly. The two hemispheres appear nearly separate (due to a large fissure down the middle of the brain), but they are connected by a band of fibers called the corpus callosum. The corpus callosum is made up of a band of axons, the part of a neuron that is in charge of sending information to other brain cells. Like a bridge of sorts, the corpus callosum is what allows the left hemisphere to communicate with the right hemisphere.

Although the idea of being "right-brained" or "left-brained" is antiquated, the two hemispheres *do* specialize in different ways of thinking. This idea might serve as a good reminder for teachers—that the unique brains in their classroom specialize in different ways of thinking too. There are students who need a holistic grasp of the big picture (right hemisphere) before hanging onto the parts, just as there are students whose need for linear, sequential (left hemisphere) instruction trumps other methods (see Figure 1.2).

CORTEX

The covering over the hemispheres looks like a wrinkled blanket. These folds and undulations are called sulci (the grooves) and gyri (the bumps) and the covering is the cortex. The cortex is six layers thick and packed with nerve cells called neurons (a kind of brain cell). These neurons represent the grayish appearance of the cortex and

Figure 1.2 Structures of the Brain

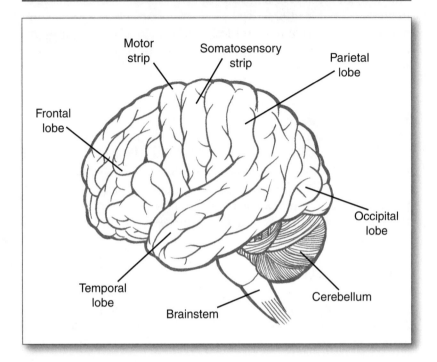

are referred to as gray matter. The cortex is wrinkled because the wrinkles allow for more surface area. If the cortex were removed and smoothed out, it would be about the size of an extra-large pizza. This allowance is needed because our brains actually grow as we learn. This information is news to many, and when it is shared, it can impact students' views of their intelligence regarding whether it is fixed or malleable.

CEREBELLUM

In the back of the brain, tucked underneath the cortex, is the cerebellum. Instead of folds and wrinkles, the cerebellum has striated tissue that looks more like muscle. It has more neurons than any other part of the brain, and it supports motor and mental dexterity. It influences our ability to balance and move, as well as different kinds of learning and memory. The cerebellum receives an enormous amount of information from other parts of the brain, and its ability to sort and process information from the cortex is as important as it is impressive. Research regarding the cerebellum playing a larger role in cognition than previously thought might be reason to view activities in school, such as physical education, with careful consideration.

BRAIN STEM

The brain stem is located in the middle of the base of the brain. It is the structure that connects the brain to the spinal cord. Functions of the brain stem include automatic functions, like breathing, the beating of the heart, and blood pressure. The functions of the brain stem are absolutely necessary to sustain life.

LOBES OF THE BRAIN

Now that I have provided a big picture (right hemispheric) of the external structures of the brain, I would like to go into a little more detail. When looking at an image of a human brain, we see certain regions, some more clearly demarcated than others. These different regions of the brain have specialized functions, and they are referred to as lobes. The different structures have different functions, from thinking skills to motor skills, from meaning making to memory retrieving. The part that is active while a person is solving an algebra problem might be different than the part that is working while a person is jogging around a track. This doesn't mean that only certain sections of the brain work at any one time. Many different areas of the brain work in concert all the time. When thoughts are occurring, a virtual constellation of pathways are involved, with several different regions lending their input. This is why, as will be discussed more later, instruction that includes visual, auditory, and kinesthetic input may be more effective.

There are four main lobes of the brain: the frontal lobes, the temporal lobes, the parietal lobes, and the occipital lobes. The motor strip and somatosensory strip are located between the parietal lobes and the frontal lobes. When we understand the functions of each lobe, we better understand why input that includes different modalities can be so effective—it is co-opting various parts of the brain, which in turn, may create more pathways of thought or recall.

FRONTAL LOBES

The location of the frontal lobes is easy to remember because they are in the front of the head, right behind the forehead. These two lobes represent about a third of the cortex and contain the prefrontal cortex, an area in charge of executive functions. That means the frontal lobes help people think in ways that include setting goals, delaying gratification, recognizing future consequences from current actions, overriding or suppressing inappropriate responses, recalling memories that are not task based, synthesizing information, and making sense of emotions. This area of the brain is the mecca of problem solving, critical thinking, and creativity.

The frontal lobes reach full maturity somewhere in the second decade. This means that many of our students in a K–12 system are not operating with a fully matured brain. This does *not* mean that children from preschool through high school don't use their frontal lobes for higher level thinking. What it does mean, however, is that the kinds of executive thinking we can depend on from adults are not always accessible to our students. There are things we can do in schools to act as surrogate frontal lobes for children. For instance, incorporating protocols for goal setting (a function of the prefrontal cortex) in classrooms can act as a scaffold for frontal lobe use. Helping students delay gratification (another function of the prefrontal cortex) by implementing routines in the classroom where students listen to peers without interruption, or take turns, is another way to assist and enlist and guide frontal lobe use.

Because the frontal lobes play such a large role in learning, memory, and higher-level thinking, educators must do what is necessary to protect these precious areas from damage, either physically or psychologically.

PARIETAL LOBES

The parietal lobes are located behind the frontal lobes and in front of the occipital lobes, across the top of the head. The parietal lobes help people integrate sensory information from their environment.

Portions of the parietal lobes are involved in visual-spatial processing, known as the "where" and "how" stream. They help people know where they are in space relative to objects that surround them, and they allow us to manipulate our bodies and objects in an effective way. This is what enables people to move through a crowded room without bumping into others along the way or to know approximately how much further one has to walk to get to the coffee shop in sight. Students who display a lack of orienting or integrating information about where their body is in space might, on the surface, simply appear to be clumsy or not "with it" in a classroom. A teacher who understands there is a specific structure in the brain related to this ability might better understand or find ways to help a student with balance or estimation by using strategies that integrate such skills, like practicing routines and procedures physically.

MOTOR STRIP

The motor cortex is located like a headband in between the frontal and parietal lobes. The motor cortex contains different sections that are responsible for various kinds of differentiated movements. Think of all the diverse ways that you move, as well as all the specific purposes for moving. It's no wonder the motor strip differentiates movement. Compare how someone might move when he or she is learning to play a game like tennis to how an avid swimmer might move. On the surface, those two activities might seem very similar, but from a motor cortex viewpoint, differentiation is critical.

Practice is one of the most effective ways to help students acquire motor skills. This is why a coach can be such an asset to someone learning how to throw a fastball or execute a double backflip. Masterful teachers know the importance of creating muscle memories, which might manifest itself by adding movement to words or phrases to help students remember, or practicing procedures in the classroom before expecting students to seamlessly apply them.

SOMATOSENSORY STRIP

The somatosensory cortex is an area of the brain that receives and processes sensations, like pain, heat, and touch. It lies just behind the motor cortex in a headband-like shape. A map exists on the somatosensory cortex, which includes touch receptors for each part of the body. This map has touch receptors that are unevenly distributed across the cortex. In certain parts, where a great deal of sensitivity to touch exists, there is a greater proportion of receptors, which means a person can feel even subtle differences in texture or vibration, like on the fingertips. Other less sensitive parts of the body show a much greater distance between touch receptors, like on the back.

TEMPORAL LOBES

The location of the temporal lobes is easy to remember because they are near our temples. The temporal lobes are extraordinarily important with regard to language, auditory processing, and memory. With regard to language, the temporal lobes help us to verbalize language as well as comprehend it. In most people, the verbalization skills, comprehension, syntax, and processing of language are positioned in the left temporal lobe, while the ability to understand tone of voice, prosody, and vocal subtleties occurs in the right temporal lobe.

When Jill Bolte Taylor, author of *Stroke of Insight* (2006), describes the morning she experienced her stroke (which affected her left hemisphere), she describes a conversation on the phone with her secretary in which she said the secretary sounded to her just like a golden retriever. She comprehended none of the meaning, grammar, or syntax of the words in the conversation, but she did pick up on the tone and prosody (her undamaged right temporal lobe at work) and was somehow able to communicate that she needed help.

Certain kinds of memory are also a specialty of the temporal lobes. Episodic memory, the kind that enables someone to remember an event or "episode"; declarative memory, the kind that enables someone to remember facts and figures; and the movement from short term to working memory are assisted by the temporal lobes. A structure called the hippocampus sits deep within the temporal lobes and plays a large role in short-term and working memory formation. There have been cases where people have had the hippocampus surgically removed, due to persistent and violent epileptic seizures, and the result was a major deficit in the ability to form new memories. Memory is discussed further in a subsequent chapter.

OCCIPITAL LOBES

The occipital lobes are the visual processing center of your brain and they enable you to see all the different shapes and colors in the world. Images and visuals are also stored as memories in the occipital lobe. The word occipital comes from the Latin words meaning "back of the head," which is a way to remember the location of these lobes. They rest right under the occipital bone of the skull.

The occipital lobes represent about a fourth of the cortex, and they are extremely efficient visual processors. When we use images along with speech, we not only enhance our audience's understanding, we enhance their recall as well. In fact, in a famous study by a man named Lionel Standing (1973) in the 1970s, participants were shown 10,000 images in a five-day period. After the five days, participants were again shown some of the originally viewed pictures, with some new pictures thrown into the mix. Subjects were able to discriminate the ones they had seen earlier from the new images about 80% of the time. The more vivid the image, the more likely they were able to recall it later. Ability to recall images in the short term averages about 90%, while the ability to recall images in the long term (months later) is about 75%. That's an incredibly effective system.

Teachers can take advantage of our highly efficient visual system by using visuals before and during instruction to help students make quick connections. For instance, when teaching a vocabulary word, finding a visual that represents that word will help students' initial understanding, as well as recall. Before teaching about a civilization, a teacher can show images of the geography, the people, and the artifacts, so students can easily and quickly tap into prior knowledge or add to their current neural networks.

CELLULAR BRAIN

Now that the structures of the brain are understood, it's time to go even deeper, to a microscopic level. The brain is made up of fat, water, and protein. There are different kinds of brain cells. For our purposes, the two important cells are neurons, which are the cells that communicate via electro-chemical messages, and glia. Glia are brain cells that act as structural supports and little nurses, taking care of the neurons. At this time, it is believed that glial cells don't communicate in the same way that neurons do, but recent research is surfacing the possibilities that glial cells play a more expanded role than support system for neurons.

Each neuron is a self-contained functioning unit. The three basic parts of a neuron are the cell body, the dendrites, which receive incoming information, and the axon, which sends outgoing information. The hand is a pretty decent model of a neuron. The palm of the hand represents the cell body, where the DNA lives. The fingers represent the dendrites, while the axon might be the forearm. A substance called myelin wraps around the axon to provide a form of insulation and acts as a superconductor. Myelin is a fatty, waxy substance that allows for optimal processing speed (see Figure 1.3).

The brain is packed with neurons, about 100 billion. When information is processed through the brain, neurons communicate with neighboring networks to create a symphony of thought. The more often certain networks are used, the more efficiently they may work. The more networks are working efficiently, the richer the neural networks may become. This information helps

Figure 1.3   The Neuron

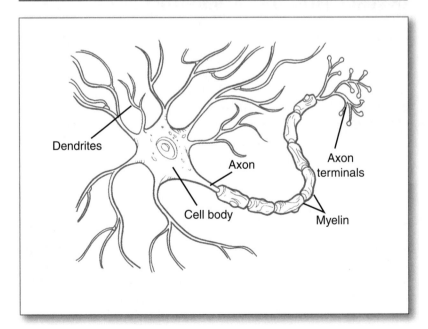

instructional leaders, teachers, and students understand that learning is an active process that is, in part, controlled by the learner. Effort, practice, and elaboration of thought might play a greater role in getting smarter than genetics. Educators have some control over things like practice and elaboration. They can engineer the environment in ways that enhance neuronal communication, and that's what learning is all about.

Understanding the structures and functions of the brain, including some of the key vocabulary, is the first step in comprehending how the brain works. Each of the subsequent chapters build upon this foundational knowledge and add new dimensions to it. This will augment the instructional leader's repertoire and comfort level when providing resources for teachers, serving as an instructional expert and communicating to colleagues or parents about our most important charge as instructional leaders—how we learn.

Understanding how the brain works, coupled with knowledge of plasticity and mindsets, provides the instructional leader with vital information when considering how to assist teachers in improving their practice.

PLASTICITY'S ROLE IN INSTRUCTIONAL LEADERSHIP

I believe that average teachers can become good teachers and good teachers can become great teachers. The same can be said of instructional leaders. I believe this because I have witnessed it throughout my career. But brain plasticity trumps this empirical evidence. Plasticity is a term used to explain how the brain can change its physiological structure. With each new learning experience, new connections are made among groups of neurons. Like sections of superhighways, these groups of neurons, called neural networks, can connect to one another in various, unique configurations. As people learn more, depth of understanding increases, and these neural networks become denser. This is why an expert in a field has less difficulty making connections between seemingly unconnected ideas. The expert has more on-ramps and off-ramps from which to pull information. These thickets of neurons and biological infrastructures result in the kind of intellectual flexibility needed to adapt and continue to think on one's feet in a new or novel context, the kind of skill that benefits teachers, students, and instructional leaders everywhere. It was once believed that the brain you are born with is the same brain you die with, but we now know this is not the case (National Research Council, 1999). Effort, hard work, and deliberate, effective practice, can improve cognitive and physical abilities. This is very good news for instructional leaders and the teachers who aspire to continue to learn and grow.

MINDSETS AND INSTRUCTIONAL LEADERSHIP

Plasticity reveals itself in different ways. People can change or develop new ways of thinking or habits of mind. The way a person views intelligence and learning has an impact upon that person's life as a learner. Plasticity, as it applies to a mindset, is revealed in the work of Carol Dweck. In her book, *Mindset—The New Psychology of Success* (2006), Dweck describes the ideas and rationale behind mindsets.

According to Dweck, people who believe that they have some power over what they do in their life tend to adopt a certain kind of mindset. Mindsets impact how people respond to challenges and how they see their brains as able to change and grow with experience—or not.

Dweck describes two polarities: the growth mindset and the fixed mindset. Those who believe their effort pays off are those that Dweck would refer to as people with growth mindsets. People who, on the other hand, believe that they are habitually powerless to events in their life, who see themselves as constant victims of circumstances, who see having to expend effort as failing before starting, are people who have fixed mindsets.

The idea that our brains are sculpted by experience is something a person who understands plasticity would recognize, and this belief aligns with growth mindsets. Another hallmark of a growth mindset is the idea that intelligence can be developed. People with growth mindsets embrace challenges, figure out how to stay the course when barriers arise, and find inspiration in the success of others.

Someone with a fixed mindset, on the other hand, believes that intelligence is fixed, that our brains are set, like concrete, with an inability to change regardless of circumstances. Fear of looking stupid is another hallmark of a fixed mindset. This fear may keep someone with a fixed mindset from asking a question to clarify, and that person may also avoid challenges or see effort as futile.

Mindsets are revealed in staffrooms and classrooms throughout our nation. Helping administrators, teachers, and students understand mindsets, how to recognize mindsets, and most importantly, how to nurture a mindset, can be incredibly helpful as our brain changes through our learning. Following are two tables that represent the evidence of the two different types of mindsets. These tables show that the instructional leader can play a role in the development of growth mindsets by implementing certain strategies.

Hallmarks of a Growth Mindset	Growing a Mindset Through . . .
Sees challenges as exciting	Supporting teachers in efforts that present a challenge
Persists through barriers	Assisting teachers in problem solving through barriers
Sees effort as a necessary component to mastery	Measuring progress and providing evidence of such
Learns from criticism	Finding ways to give feedback effectively
Hallmarks of a Fixed Mindset	**Fixing a Mindset Through . . .**
Avoids challenges	Pointing out failures of the past
Gives up easily	Taking away control and choice
Sees effort as fruitless	Not recognizing efforts and their impact on students
Ignores Feedback	Providing feedback in ways that promote defensiveness

HOW MIGHT THE INSTRUCTIONAL LEADER SUPPORT A TEACHER STRUGGLING WITH THESE PRINCIPLES?

A vital part of an instructional leader's skill set includes assisting teachers with the process of continually improving their practice, and an extra measure of urgency is added when a teacher is struggling. After each chapter, several resources are included that the instructional leader can use to (a) quantify teachers' understanding and implementation of principles, (b) provide teachers with ideas for implementing effective methods, and (c) measure teachers' progress as they increase their understanding about the brain-compatible principles therein. Aside from the use of these tools, there are methods that can be included in the instructional leader's repertoire that will help to promote growth among the teachers.

CELEBRATE WHAT YOU WANT TO SEE MORE OF

It's important for teachers to understand when they are becoming more effective (Marzano, 2003). One way to help teachers do this, after quantifying practice in some way (through the use of a rubric), is to mark the progress made and celebrate it. Finding links between the improved practice of teachers and the improved achievement of students is one of the most relevant and meaningful ways to do this. For instance, if a teacher has made a conscious effort to improve his practice with regard to memory systems, an instructional leader might ask that teacher to collect student work that will serve to indicate their ability to recall information from a content area, and then help the teacher find evidence of this in the student work. As teachers find evidence of improved recall, they need to ensure that it is celebrated in some way. This can be done, for example, by making a statement that clearly establishes the good that has come out of the teacher's learning: (a) "Seventy-six percent of your students have increased their engagement in learning tasks due to the fact that they have internalized the morning procedures in your classroom," or (b) "This science quiz shows that 26 out of 30 students recalled the rock cycle with 100% accuracy." These statements are filled with the reasons many teachers are committed to their profession.

By articulating what she wants to see more of, the instructional leader positively impacts her own practice, her teachers' practices, and the general instructional climate of the school.

USING THE SURVEY

Feedback can elevate, motivate, and facilitate learning, and this is expanded upon later in the book. Following is a survey that could be used in several different ways. It would be a good idea to simply read the five questions that apply to each of the chapters as they are approached in the reading. The questions can act as a priming tool or allow for a gauge of prior knowledge on any given chapter. I would recommend a return to these questions after reading to measure progress in gaining information from the chapters. Alternatively, there might be a specific section in the book, for example, that is most relevant when beginning a new school year, and you might have your staff take a look at the questions to gauge their current knowledge level or understanding of the topic.

SURVEY FOR BRAIN-COMPATIBLE INSTRUCTIONAL LEADERSHIP

Disagree   Agree

1   2   3   4   5

Chapter 1—A Brain Primer

1. I can locate the basic structures of the human brain.

2. I can explain the basic structures and functions of the human brain.

3. I understand the role neurons play in the brain.

4. I can show why understanding how the brain works can help an instructional leader.

5. I understand the concepts of plasticity and mindsets and how they relate to educators.

Chapter 2—Emotions

1. I can communicate vital information regarding emotions and learning to my teaching staff.

2. I understand how positive and negative emotional responses can impact learning.

3. I can share strategies about creating emotionally relevant learning experiences for students.

4. I can recognize a lesson that takes advantage of the beneficial emotions.

5. I can help a teacher plan learning experiences that elicit positive emotions.

Chapter 3—Attention and Engagement

1. I can describe the relationship between attention and engagement.

2. I can share strategies that help gain a student's attention with teachers.

3. I can share strategies that help engage a learner with teachers.

4. I can recognize attention and engagement in a classroom observation.

5. I can assist a teacher in planning with qualities of engaging work in mind.

Chapter 4—The Power of Processing

1. I can communicate the relationship between neural networks and processing.

2. I can share information with my staff about what factors enhance processing.

3. I can apply my understanding about processing to my work as an instructional leader.

4. I can analyze a lesson plan for adequate processing protocols.

5. I can apply the information about processing to what I observe during instruction.

Chapter 5—Feedback

1. I can describe what is going on in the brain when a person receives feedback.

2. I can analyze a lesson plan for elements of effective feedback.

3. I can share strategies with others regarding ways to provide feedback.

4. I can recognize and record effective feedback practices during instruction.

5. I can effectively give feedback to teachers.

Chapter 6—Memory

1. I understand the difference between declarative and non-declarative memory systems.

2. I understand the three different phases of memory (short term, working, and long term).

3. I can describe some things that inhibit robust memory formation in a classroom.

4. I can describe some strategies that enhance memory in a classroom.

5. I can evaluate a lesson in terms of attention to memory.

CHAPTER SUMMARY

The human brain is an incredibly complex organ. Although the brain works in concert, there are some structures that have specialized functions. First, there are the hemispheres, one left and one right. Each hemisphere specializes in certain ways of thinking and dealing with the world. The cortex is the "wrapping" or bark of the brain. It is where the gray matter (composed of neurons) exists. The cerebellum is a structure that controls balance and movement, among other things. The brain stem's function is to promote automatic functions, like breathing and the beating of the heart.

There are four lobes of the brain and two strips within those lobes that serve several functions. The frontal lobes, which contain the prefrontal cortex, help us with executive functions such as critical thinking, goal setting, and delaying gratification. The parietal lobes are in charge of the perception people have of their body in space. The motor strip is a piece of cortical real estate behind the frontal lobes and serves as the area that helps people move their bodies, while the somatosensory strip handles how people perceive physical sensations, like whether something is hot or cold, sharp or dull. The temporal lobes deal with language, hearing, and memory, and the occipital lobes handle sight.

On a cellular level, the brain is composed of fat, protein, and water. Neurons are brain cells that communicate with others in order to form thoughts and actions. Neurons fire and wire together, creating neural paths, or networks, that serve as cognitive maps for use in thinking or remembering.

Plasticity is the term used to explain how the brain changes as a result of the environment. What was once believed to be an unchanging organ is now known to be a dynamic and responsive one. This means we can become smarter, more adept, and better practitioners, with the help of effort, practice, and mindsets.

POSTASSESSMENT CHAPTER 1—A BRAIN PRIMER

1. I can locate the basic structures (lobes) of the human brain.

2. I can explain the basic functions of the human brain.

3. I understand the role neurons play in the brain.

4. I can explain why a teacher might want to consider using more than one mode of input.

5. I can explain why assessing using different modalities might be beneficial.

QUESTIONS FOR STUDY GROUP

1. Do teachers take full advantage of their students' visual processing abilities? How might teachers enhance their learning and recall through visual input?

2. The executive functions of the frontal lobe are critical for thoughtful, mature actions. What protocols or procedures are in place that might help students' frontal lobes to develop fully?

3. How might the information in this chapter assist teachers in teaching more effectively?

CHAPTER 2

Emotions' Impact on Learning

*Children will work harder and do things—even odd things
like adding fractions—for people they love and trust.*

—Nel Noddings (1988, p. 32)

Students and teachers come to us with a wide range of emotional intelligence and aptitude. Some have had guidance in gaining knowledge and skills to effectively deal with emotions. Some know how to calm themselves, how to listen with empathy, or how to deflect an insulting remark. There are methods to employ that assist people in gaining emotional competence, a skill that will positively impact their cognition, their relationships, and their communication. The instructional leader will learn how emotions impact thinking and gain methods that evoke helpful emotions in classrooms and staffrooms.

This chapter illustrates things an instructional leader wants to see or combat in classrooms or staffrooms, shares methods for healthy communication and supervision, and provides the instructional leader with tools to measure progress and support teachers in their efforts to understand and implement these ideas in their practice.

Emotional valence is a term used by neuroscientists when talking about the emotional environment. Similar to in science when a molecule has a positive or negative charge, an environment can be positively or negatively charged. This is how the term *valence* will be used for the remainder of this chapter.

Have you ever . . .

- *Been publicly insulted and not been able to think of a comeback—until you were in the shower the next day?*
- *Become motivated and engaged in a learning event because it was emotionally positive?*
- *Been put on the spot with a question that you couldn't answer even though you had the correct information?*

HOW INSULTS AFFECT THINKING

Nearly everyone has experienced a cutting remark that left them stunned. Not only is the person left speechless, she might be subjected to a persistent replay of the insult throughout the day, which demands attention that could be given to a more productive endeavor. It can frustrate and impact mood, decision making, and thinking.

Emotions are responsible for one's sudden deficiency of wit during such events. It's no different for the student who is the recipient of a stinging comment by a teacher or for the teacher getting slammed by an angry parent in an Individual Education Plan meeting. Regardless of age or context, the neurological system at work in these cases is basically the same (LeDoux, 1996).

THE TRANSFORMATIVE POWER OF POSITIVE EMOTIONS

Anyone who has seen another experience an "aha" moment has witnessed the power of positive emotions. During these moments, there is usually an undeniable physical response by the learner. This response might manifest itself in facial expression, body language, or vocal gesticulations. During these events, the brain's pleasure and reward pathways light up. This example is used for two reasons. One is to underscore the idea that positive emotional experiences don't require a cheerleader standing by, coaxing bliss out of a situation. The other is to illustrate that one of the natural by-products of learning is a positive emotional state. This is one of the reasons that instructional leaders want to be equipped to ferret out the classrooms where students enjoy a consistently positive climate. These might be the classrooms with the most robust learning going on. Studies build a strong case for how positive emotions enhance learning, and instructional leaders witness it empirically every day (Caine et al., 2009; Sousa, 2010; Willis, 2010).

HOW ANXIETY CAN CURTAIL CLEAR THINKING

This might be observed in a classroom of students or in an adult learning situation—someone is called upon to answer a question and doesn't. There are a few different things that may be impairing the reticent participant. One may be that he doesn't know the answer. Another culprit is anxiety; when we are anxious, our ability to process effectively is hampered. In a classroom, anxiety can impact student learning and desire to attend class. Principals and teachers may do things that provoke anxiety or quell it. This chapter examines some things instructional leaders may do and share with their staff to promote a positive emotional valence while concurrently curtailing negative emotions in their schools.

THE LIMBIC REGION—THE ROLE OF THE AMYGDALA AND HIPPOCAMPUS

Deep within the brain there is an area called the limbic region, which contains an arrangement of structures that process emotions. The amygdala is one of these structures. It's like an emotional soldier, guarding the brain's gate. It continually assesses whether our world is harmful or safe, painful or pleasurable (Wolfe, 2010).

The amygdala works with another structure—the hippo-campus. The hippocampus, Latin for sea horse, is shaped like the tail of its name and plays a role in memory formation. These structures work together to inform and help us remember. We remember events that might hamper or enhance survival because the amygdala adds extra vividness to certain events and tells the hippocampus, *"Hey, we need to remember to stay away from that person—we almost didn't survive that verbal attack,"* or *"We need to remember how good it feels to solve problems—we were able to help the whole class understand equations better today"* (Wolfe, 2010).

The functions and relationship between the amygdala and the hippocampus are why students quickly recognize and remember which teachers seem like friends and which seem like foes, which classrooms feel safe and which feel threatening. As shown in Figure 2.1, the amygdala and hippocampus sit right next to each other in the brain.

Figure 2.1   The Amygdala and Hippocampus

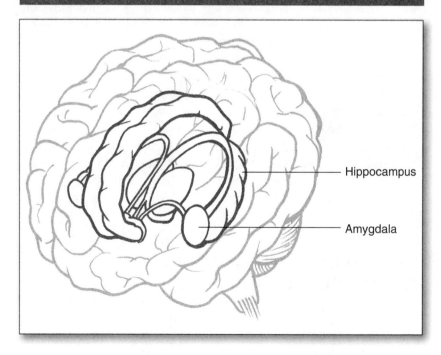

FAST VS. SLOW PATHWAY (FIGHT OR FLIGHT VS. THOUGHTFUL RESPONSE)

When the amygdala finds something that might hamper survival, it springs into action. Sometimes it works a bit prematurely, such as when people are hiking and jump when they see a stick, because they initially perceive the stick as a snake. This happens because of the two pathways that our brains have developed, as described by LeDoux (2010): the slow and thoughtful pathway and the fast and impetuous pathway.

The slow pathway allows information to pass through all of the neural structures and channels (in microseconds), including the very important cortex, where people think, plan, ponder, make decisions, and thoughtfully respond. This is an extremely important point to remember. The usage of the slow pathway is why people don't jump when they see a real snake behind the glass case in the zoo. The human brain is given the full benefit of time, safety, and the prefrontal cortex. The slow pathway is the route we want our students and teachers brains to be taking in school, because it is this pathway that co-opts the frontal lobes and the prefrontal cortex, the area of the brain that provides the ability to use the essential executive functions needed for success in school and life, like critical thinking, planning, and reflection.

The fast pathway is invoked when someone goes into a fight-or-flight situation. When a person becomes highly emotionally charged, as in the case of a survival encounter, the reticular activating system shuts down the cerebral cortex and the fight-or-flight response kicks in. During this response, our bodies proceed on "automatic pilot" where instinct and survival take over. When the threat decreases and relaxation increases, the limbic system retreats, and the reticular activating system (RAS) turns the cortex back on, which permits critical thinking, creativity, and reasoning to return as well (Carter, 2009).

NEGATIVE EMOTIONS' IMPACT IN A SCHOOL SETTING

What does this have to do with school? In school, social situations can be survival encounters. Bullies could be a reason some students are in a fixed state of emotional arousal, one that is sapping their cognition, especially from their prefrontal cortex (Wolfe, 2010). If heading to the playground conjures up thoughts of survival for students, their ability to find math engaging is probably going to be compromised. Being admonished by a teacher in a tone that they find frightening, a tardy policy requiring students to be isolated from their peers, children being asked to read aloud when they aren't yet able to, might also create a breeding ground for students shifting to the fast pathway. These might not be life or death survival encounters, but they can often result in the same kinds of physiological responses as a real survival encounter might elicit.

POSITIVE EMOTIONS IN A SCHOOL SETTING

During a positive emotional experience, the brain releases chemicals that grease the tracks for increased cognition; people get a boost from neurotransmitters that aid in mood stabilization, motivation, and joy (Diamond, 2010). Neurotransmitters are chemicals that the body makes to help neurons process. During these events, the pleasure pathway of the brain gets involved and we experience pleasure that shows up on our face. These emotions can be a bit contagious for others because of mirror neurons. Positive emotions assist learning, retention of what has been learned, and a person's ability to access the very important prefrontal cortex (Csikszentmihalyi, 1990; Diamond, 2009).

It is no wonder that the most effective teachers are often those that consistently elicit positive emotional responses from students (Danielson, 2007; Strong, Tucker, & Hindman, 2004,). When people feel good, they want to repeat that feeling. One of the best bits of news for the instructional leader is that the brain is hardwired to feel good upon solving a problem, learning something new, or completing a challenging task. When students easily recognize how their learning equips them to solve meaningful problems, the learning is approached with the kind of fervor and positive emotional responses we see in classrooms of our most effective teachers. For instance, when students understand that their ability to order the accurate amount of material for a real-world project, say, building a garden bed, lies in their ability to accurately solve certain kinds of math problems, meaning, engagement, and interest in the task are heightened (Caine et al., 2009; VanDeWeghe, 2009). So, in light of this information, what are some things instructional leaders might look for and do to ensure students are protected from harmful negative emotional responses while receiving the benefits of positive emotional responses at school?

POSITIVE EMOTIONAL VALENCE IN A CLASSROOM

In this next section, three big ideas that are unavoidably linked to the emotional valence in a classroom are examined. These three big ideas are relationships, the nature of the work students are doing, and the classroom climate. As an instructional leader, these three dimensions provide a breadth of knowledge about the potential effectiveness in the classroom (Hattie, 2009; Marzano, 2003; Schlechty, 2002).

Relationships

The relationship between a teacher and a student is critical; positive interactions among teacher and students are a vital component of effective teaching (Marzano, 2003). Positive interactions can grow through small, simple things that occur in the context of teaching, things like giving students a voice in classroom policies, communicating with care, and planning learning experiences that are meaningful and relevant to students. Teachers who are honest and earnest about their role as a teacher and communicate the importance of student learning engender an effective and positive teacher–student relationship.

Respect is the cornerstone of positive interactions at school. Teachers who consistently model this powerful mood stabilizer in classrooms where students show respect to the teacher, their peers, and themselves, are emotionally positive classrooms where learning is heightened (Danielson, 2007; Martin & Downson, 2009).

The way a teacher deals with student misconduct can model healthy emotional responses and strengthen relationships with students. Dealing with misconduct in a firm, fair, and consistent way sends a message that every student's learning is important and will not be sacrificed. Teachers can choose to craft expectations of behavior with students or share already-formed norms of the classroom with students; either way, these expectations should elicit positive emotional responses from both groups. Most students want clear and consistent expectations, and if the teacher bends or switches the rules for some students without any rationale, student trust may erode.

The saying, "Kids don't care what you know until they know that you care," sums up why building good relationships with students is one of the most important steps in teaching. Evidence of respectful, caring relationships is one of the most important elements in a school, and it is something an instructional leader should seek and encourage (Sousa, 2010).

The Nature of the Work Students Are Doing

This section builds a bit on the previous section. The nature of the work students do in a classroom depends a great deal on the teacher's ability and commitment to planning and instruction. As competent a teacher may be in delivering instruction, the more important element to consider is the nature of the work students are being asked to learn and engage in at school. In fact, one of the keys to the success of a school is developed through the creation of engaging, relevant, complex schoolwork for students (Daggett, 2008; Jensen, 2006; Schlechty, 2002).

Our brains were designed for complex problem solving—solving problems recruits pleasure pathways in our brains (Carpenter, 2008; Lambert, 2008), thus eliciting positive emotions. Knowing this, it makes sense to ask students to enlist the kind of challenging thinking, decision making, and collaborating it takes to solve real-world problems.

A classroom where students are given opportunities to learn in differentiated ways, where diverse methods for input, processing, and assessment are used, where the students' worlds are weaved into the curriculum, where what students are learning is relevant and rigorous, where fun is not forgotten and where students have a voice—that classroom most likely elicits positive emotions. On the other hand, classrooms where the majority of work stems from disconnected worksheets that place learning discrete skills above a juicy question to investigate, or problem to solve, or a story to tell—these are classrooms where the nature of the work students are doing lacks emotionality and probably engagement.

The nature of the work students are doing will surface when they are asked questions about it. When students can answer questions that require them to explain the purpose of their learning and how it might help them, or someone else, in the future, this is a good litmus test for relevant work. Let's say you are in a classroom where students are learning how to add a "hook" to their writing. You approach a student and ask what he thinks is the purpose of this learning. If the student can articulate that by adding a good hook to his writing he can grab the reader's attention, which will encourage further reading and ultimately accomplish his mission of sharing his writing and self-expression with a larger audience, this is evidence that the work has some relevance for the student.

In the tables at the end of the chapter there are more suggestions about the kinds of things an instructional leader might look for in terms of the nature and structure of student work that promote positive emotions in the classroom (see Tables 2.1–2.6).

Classroom Climate

Both relationships and the nature of work students are doing serve as a conduit for a positive classroom climate, but there's still more to add to this amalgam that can either promote productive, energetic learning or lethargic, apathetic compliance. Classroom climate is like the weather in a classroom. It can be dark and stormy or sunny with a light breeze. Things an instructional leader wants to pay attention to with regard to the classroom climate are the language used, the classroom norms of behavior, and the aesthetics of the classroom.

Language

The way people talk to one another can powerfully impact emotions. Language actually shapes thoughts, feelings, and experiences (Vygotsky, 1978). Classrooms where student and teacher language is thoughtful and positive are classrooms where students feel more confident about taking intellectual risks, being creative, and collaborating (Denton, 2007). Teachers can embed ways of talking that model the use of positive language. For instance, teachers may use positive presuppositions in their communication with students, peers, and parents. Positive presuppositions assume that the people with whom you communicate have the best of intentions. So a positive presupposition assumes the positive. Let's say a student did not do his homework. A teacher using a positive presupposition might respond by saying, "Something out of the ordinary must have happened last night to prevent you from completing your homework. Is everything OK?" This assumes that the intention of the student was to complete the task. A negative presupposition might sound more like this: "Last night's homework got in the way of free time, eh?" When teachers frame their communication through the lens of positive presuppositions, it can engender both trust and respect on the part of students and parents. In her book, *The Power of Our Words,* Paula Denton (2007) describes teacher language that helps children learn. Active listening, asking open-ended questions, using reinforcing language, and redirecting language are all aspects of language that positively shape the classroom climate.

The way students speak in the classroom sheds light on the climate. Students who speak to one another with respect, in both content and tone, engender positive communication and emotions. Sometimes students need to be directly taught ways to communicate positively, through modeling, teaching, and activities that help students understand and practice how to disagree with one another or acquire information from a peer in a positive way (Glenn, 1990).

Norms of Behavior

The norms of behavior in a classroom can speak volumes to the instructional leader. As mentioned earlier, regardless of whether the norms were developed collaboratively with students or simply shared on the first day as classroom expectations, norms are what help students incorporate effective ways of learning and dealing with one another as well as hold everyone accountable for certain behaviors in a classroom. The norms should be known, shown, and internalized by every child in the class, as well as the teacher and any visitors to the class. This might mean they are posted in an obvious area of the classroom as a reminder. Norms can also be revisited by the teacher or other members of the classroom when or if needed, thereby making them a working document. For instance, at the beginning of the school year, when students and teacher are getting to know each other and how their classroom is going to function, the norms might include an idea about ensuring that everyone's voice is heard. After several months, it is obvious to all that every student has internalized this norm, and it might be replaced with a more sophisticated version of it, such as ensuring the speaker provides suggestions for improvement if bringing a complaint to the table. As the climate and culture of a classroom changes, norms can change too.

Class meetings can promote the norms of behavior in a classroom. A brief explanation of the protocol for class meetings is provided in the sample observation near the end of this chapter.

Aesthetics of the Classroom

The aesthetics of the classroom is the last of the three big ideas that relate to the emotional valence of a classroom. Regardless of age, people respond emotionally to the space they inhabit. The human brain is hardwired to appreciate space to move around in, as well as an aesthetically pleasing environment (Haslam & Knight, 2010). Where people spend time can impact their emotional states, which in turn can impact their cognition.

Imagine being back in school as a student and walking into two different classrooms. One classroom is arranged with the student in mind. Upon entering, you are filled with a feeling of anticipation. Desks are arranged in trios and movable, to allow students to structure groups of varying sizes. Natural light fills the space from a bank of windows along the length of the room, which enables better vision. The bulletin boards that adorn the walls include a balance of interesting images, student work, and white space, which allows the eye to rest. There is a clean and spacious feel to the classroom. There is space on counters and bookcases for students to use as an impromptu desk if needed, and a few plants evoke a relaxed atmosphere. The room is neat and comfortable and it seems the teacher who lives here must care about his surroundings. One might infer that he also cares about the people who inhabit it.

Now let's walk into the second classroom. This classroom, unlike the first one, evokes a feeling of disappointment. Desks are in no particular order; some are bunched up near the wall while others are separated from one another, gathering dust in the corners. The curtains are drawn, which necessitates the use of every fluorescent light in the room and eliminates any natural light or view of outside. The counters are cluttered with boxes, stacks of papers, books, and files, making it impossible to use any horizontal space other than the 3.2 square feet of desk space allotted to each student. The walls are, for the most part, empty, except for where the occasional wire or old thumbtack rests. There are a few pieces of information taped to the cabinet in the front of the room regarding safety proto-col in an emergency and two pieces of student work stuck to a small bulletin board in back—incomplete work with no names. The room looks messy, like whoever lives here doesn't care much about it.

Our surroundings evoke emotions. Teachers and the students within their classroom can choose what kinds of emotions the room evokes—that of care, value, thoughtfulness, or that of indif-ference, deficiency, or thoughtlessness. It takes little time and effort to create the former and the payoff is undeniably constructive.

Understanding how our environment impacts our emotions helps the instructional leader inform and expect the kinds of class-room atmospheres that can support optimal student mood and performance (Moore, 2009).

Now that you have been given the opportunity to examine what to look for in classrooms that indicate a positive emotional valence, the following section describes practices and skills an instructional leader can put into place that may stimulate positive emotional responses with the adults at a school site.

MODELING OF HEALTHY EMOTIONAL RESPONSES

What do emotionally competent instructional leaders model? Think of the responses they hope to see in their staff: habits of mind that help teachers persist through challenges, ability to put the brakes on behavior or language that might be emotionally damaging, ability to empathize in order to understand another's perspective, and so forth. When instructional leaders model behav-iors like these, the mirror neurons of their staff are hard at work.

On the flip side, we all know of educational leaders that model unhealthy responses—people who rant and rave; who respond to stressors with hostility, sarcasm, impatience, or anger; who blame others; or whose default position is that of victim. Instructional lead-ers need to understand that these kinds of behaviors and responses teach their staff as much as any predetermined, intentional, professional development experience. One of the jobs of instructional leaders is to purge their campus of such responses.

LANGUAGE'S LINK TO EMOTIONS

The power of words can transform a person's day; words can uplift or destroy, encourage or discourage, animate or silence.

Have you ever been in a meeting when language positively shifted the energy in the room? This occurred in the Ontario Montclair school district, during a student study team meeting, where the child of focus was going down a worrisome path. He was cutting school three times a week, doing drugs, and hanging around with a dangerous crowd. As the people affiliated with his case entered the room, anxiety mounted and it appeared that the mother of the child grew more frightened with each entering adult. The expert outreach consultant, Newell Canfield, observed this phenomenon and quickly used language to assuage the fears and tension of everyone in the room. His voice was calm and low, his tone one of reason, importance, and earnestness. His words beautifully conveyed the group's common purpose in meeting—to attend to the dangerous behaviors of a child. Newell's language included positive presuppositions, as he relayed, without ambiguity, that everyone in the room held the common goal of helping this boy. He used pronouns like "us" and "we" in place of "I," "he," or "she" when he could. He built a sense of community in a 90-second message. The emotional valence of the room went from anxiety and fear to clarity and purpose, and it was achieved through language.

In this scenario, it was the language that had the biggest impact in changing the emotions from unproductive to productive, from negative to positive. Language shapes our experiences. It can improve the quality of one's day; it can act as a salve or a wound to an individual or an entire group. When it acts as a wound, the effects can be devastating and irrevocable. When it acts as a salve, the effects can be transformative. The words chosen by instructional leaders can have a tremendous impact on others' moods and emotional stability; therefore, the language chosen, along with its delivery, is a critical component to the skill set of an instructional leader. Following are some attributes of effective language and communication that elicit positive emotions.

Elements of Positive Language

- Body language that mimics the message—anything other than this confuses the audience/participants and puts them on edge. For instance, if people are talking about how excited they are to be working on a project, but their body language "says" something different—they are standing with arms crossed, have a furrowed brow, and speak with an anxious tone of voice—this will result in confusion for the audience.

- Tone that is either credible or approachable—pay careful attention to tone. Think of how a doctor may speak when explaining an important surgical procedure or how an accountant speaks when explaining why someone has to pay more in taxes than expected. This is a credible voice. The tone is usually calm and lowers at the end of the sentence or statement. For the approachable voice, on the other hand, think of how a colleague might ask about a recent vacation or how a friend might talk when planning an upcoming party.

- Use of inclusive words "we" and "us" instead of "I," and "he," "she," and so forth.

- Use of positive presuppositions—begin or embed statements using language that expresses your belief that everyone involved has pure intentions and acts accordingly.

- An absence of sarcasm.

- Clarity of message.

- Sincerity.

- Active listening—a person who is actively listening is listening with the intent to understand the speaker (not to figure out what the best retort will be). When people actively listen, certain body language results; they turn toward the speaker, often make direct eye contact, lean in, nod to signify understanding, and so forth. After actively listening, a person is able to accurately paraphrase the speaker without "parrot phrasing."

- Articulate paraphrasing that captures the essence of the speaker's message—this means that the listener is actively making connections about the speaker's content and can rephrase the message in his or her own words without using the speaker's exact words. This helps to ensure communication is clear to both parties.

• Clarifying questions used to ensure accuracy in communication—a clarifying question might be asked when something is said that the listener is not sure has been understood correctly. A few clarifying stems include the following: "Could you tell me a little more about . . . ?" "Help me understand . . . ." "I'm not sure I'm clear about . . . ."

EMOTIONS AND SUPERVISING TEACHERS

Now that you understand how fear impacts our cognition, you'll see how that might relate to the supervision of teachers. Some teachers are natural performers and find a walk-through or formal observation a treat. Conversely, there are teachers who become extremely anxious in instances of observation. Instructional leaders observing teaching may see evidence of this in a teacher that stumbles over his speech or forgets important elements of a lesson due to an overload of emotion. This, in turn, impacts student comfort level. Mirror neurons are at work again; when a teacher is uncomfortable, students can become uncomfortable. In addition, the frontal lobes of teachers, that same area that is in charge of executive functions, might not be getting the fuel they need during an observation that teachers respond to with fear or anxiety.

During observations such as these, the data the instructional leader collects does not offer a complete picture of a teacher's ability or student learning. And what are observations for, if not to collect real-time, authentic data for teachers to reflect upon and measure their own practice and professional growth? So what can an instructional leader do about this?

First, let's assume that the instructional leader has a trusting relationship with her staff. Trust is a powerful antidote to fear. Another is knowledge. Every teacher on the instructional leader's staff needs to not only be aware of, but become an expert in, the tools used to measure teacher competence and progress, whether that means a quick walk-through form, an informal observation form, or a formal observation form. The explicit teaching and reflection of the contents of the tools provide information that will be helpful in allaying fears, and they give a forum for dialogue about the content and purpose and how and when they will be used. If facilitated with care, this kind of dialogue can make the difference between a staff becoming resistant or resilient. When teachers feel that they have a good understanding of the content, purpose, and way a protocol will be used, they become empowered and potentially motivated (Garmston & Wellman, 2009).

However, instructional leaders may still have reticent staff members, even after a thorough investigation of the supervisory tools. This could be for a variety of reasons: teachers may like the old tool better; they may be fearful, not about the observation itself, but about their own ability to live up to the expectations of a 4 on the observation rubric. In that case, they might need support. An instructional coach, a colleague, or a mentor might be able to provide it. Through staff development, planning conversations, cognitive coaching, professional learning communities, lesson study, and reflection, support can be provided in a variety of ways through a variety of resources.

The most important and helpful thing an instructional leader can do to help alleviate fears of observation is to make it a norm to be in classrooms often, even if only for a short walk-through each day. This serves a few purposes. One relates to the key roles of an instructional leader, that of being a visible presence. It also keeps the instructional leader's finger on the pulse of what is going on in classrooms, and it clearly communicates the priorities of the instructional leader. Lastly, if teachers experience multiple visits in their classroom, the fear response can gradually loosen its grip, allowing future experiences to take place in the (slow pathway) prefrontal cortex as opposed to the (fast pathway) limbic region (LeDoux, 2010).

SCHOOLWIDE STRUCTURES THAT PROMOTE POSITIVE EMOTIONAL VALENCE

Professional learning communities (PLCs) bring emotional relevance to the workplace for administrators and teachers. Effective PLCs begin by establishing norms and working agreements, discovering common goals and values, and forming healthy relationships where their vision can manifest. This promotes an emotional landscape of openness, honesty, curiosity, care for one another, and care for students—a breeding ground for happiness and productivity (DuFour, Eaker, & DuFour, 2005).

DuFour, Eaker, DuFour, and many others have developed a training for PLCs that reflects a thoughtful example of how emotion impacts learning and how a guided approach can build, encourage, sustain, and continuously improve our capabilities as educators. Imagine an fMRI that shows the brain's activity during an episode of happiness. The areas of high activity in that fMRI are in the frontal lobes, the place where problem solving lives. Isn't that the area we want teachers to access or reside in the majority of the time? People need to feel emotionally safe in order to go there, and the concepts behind PLCs offer that safety.

If structures from organizations such as Adaptive Schools are embedded and implemented in PLCs, the level of assurance that the group will progress in its effectiveness and improve increases (Garmston & Wellman, 2009). The work of Adaptive Schools considers emotional valence from the start. The group's communication structures include an array of principles, methods, and strategies designed to ensure everyone's voice is heard, positive presuppositions are the norm, a sense of collective responsibility grows, and people always come first. A concern for the emotional safety of the individuals in the group, as well as the group as a whole, is ever-present. The other message is that our work is about student needs and what we do makes an impact. These structures represent brain-compatible and professional ways to communicate and problem solve in an educational setting.

PROFESSIONAL DEVELOPMENT ON EMOTIONS—INFORM AND TEACH

An important step in increasing a school's productive emotional valence is by helping adults understand the impact emotions have on learning. Informing teachers about how high levels of fear, anger, or other negative emotions block students' access to higher level thinking, as well as how happiness can unlock their access to critical thinking and creativity, is vital.

Once teachers understand the pernicious effects negative emotions have on learning, their curiosity is peeked regarding how to ensure that their own and their students' brains co-opt the slow pathway, especially at times when critical thinking is in order. Sharing information about how emotions affect learners, and using visuals, like what is produced when using functional magnetic resonance imaging (fMRI), can lead to thoughtful dialogue, reflection, and action on the parts of adults at school sites. This can also lead to revised norms of behavior in classrooms and staffrooms.

CONNECTING INSTRUCTIONAL LEADER KNOWLEDGE AND SKILL SETS TO EMOTIONS' IMPACT ON LEARNING

Resource Provider

When instructional leaders understand how emotions impact learning, they are more equipped to notice teachers that might benefit from learning more about the topic, or corrective feedback, because they are able to recognize aspects of negative emotional valence, name it, and speak to the destructive effects of it. Therefore, finding resources for teachers who need support in this area is a critical function of instructional leaders who possess the skill of resource providers. The instructional leader can use information from the tables at the end of the chapter to increase emotional quotient (EQ) in the classroom; those same resources can also help guide teachers' understanding of the topic.

Instructional Resource

In this chapter, the reader has learned about the importance of relevance, emotionality, and engagement with regard to emotionally positive learning experiences. This is important information for the instructional leader to communicate with teachers about, as well as recognize, during observations. This information, along with the resources at the end of the chapter, will help the instructional leader analyze lessons and assist teachers to plan lessons, using the need for relevance and emotionality as a lens from which to build learning experiences for students. The instructional leader will be more equipped to recognize, archive, and give feedback regarding instruction in classrooms that meets the requirements of positive emotional valence as well.

Good Communicator

The power of communication can serve to assuage fear, build confidence, and motivate a team. The instructional leader who understands how emotions impact learning understands that the language used can provide assurance and understanding or derail a conversation. Therefore clear, careful, and deliberate use of language is necessary. Conveying messages in ways that elicit openness and trust is imperative. Sharing information with staff regarding how emotions impact learning is helpful. Recognizing the kind of language and communication that elicits healthy emotional valences, the instructional leader can respond and teach about how emotions impact learning on the spot, with teachers or students.

SAMPLE OBSERVATION OF HOW A TEACHER EMBEDS THE PRINCIPLE

Teacher: 4th grade

Subject and time of day: First 20 minutes of the school day

Learning Target: The student will physically and mentally prepare for the day in school

Time observed: 8:00–8:20

8:00—The principal walks into the classroom and immediately notices the purposeful actions of every child in the room. It is obvious students have internalized the routines and procedures of the morning in their classroom. Students place their magnet on "hot lunch" or "sack lunch" as the recorder for the week marks the paperwork for the office. The curtains are open and the morning sunlight illuminates the room, providing plenty of natural light. The room is neat, cheerful, and filled with student work that includes art work, written stories, math exemplars, and lab write-ups. *The pleasing aesthetics of the classroom promote a sense of motivation and inclusivity and foster positive emotional responses for students.* Students are retrieving folders from a file on the counter, some individually, some in pairs or trios. The teacher is checking in with a student whose grandmother recently died. Talking is minimal among students; there is an air of purposeful action among them. Students examine the contents of their folders and choose artifacts to place on the bulletin board. All students "own" a portion of the board to display their work, and today they get to choose which work to display for the week. *Students see their work as important and useful and worthy of sharing with a broader audience than the teacher alone. This promotes a sense of relevance and meaning for the work.* Upon posting their work, students find a spot in a circle on the floor. Soon, every child is seated, awaiting the beginning of their morning ritual. *__Elapsed time 5 minutes__*

8:05—After the teacher smiles and says, "Good morning Phillip," Phillip looks at the white board and sees a prompt the teacher wrote. It says, "My morning was . . . because . . . and I'm checking in." Phillip says, "My morning was disappointing because my dad left on a business trip and didn't wake me up to tell me goodbye, and I'm checking in." *This protocol provides the student with a warm welcome from a caring adult, a chance to express an emotionally difficult feeling in order to process it and rid himself of the potential distraction and/or destruction to his cognition throughout the day.* The teacher responds to the student by paraphrasing and empathizing with him. "Sometimes when people leave on a trip and we don't have the opportunity to say goodbye it can make us feel anxious." *The use of empathic listening and paraphrasing will help the student feel heard and understood, thereby alleviating the need to perseverate on the negative emotions.* Who has a suggestion for Phillip to help him out this morning?" *The teacher models positive presuppositions that students in the classroom have the capacity to help one another with real-life problems and encourages students to act accordingly.* Another student raises her hand and mentions a strategy she has used in the past that helped her in similar occasions. She envisions what the night will be like when her parent returns and that helps her move from anxiety to excitement. This is referred to as a "state change." Phillip thanks his peer and the teacher turns to another student. "Good morning Sarah," begins the next round, where students are given the opportunity to deal with any kind of emotional baggage that might impede their ability to learn that morning

(Continued)

(Continued)

or day. The vast majority of students were able to complete the prompt with a quick response and move through the protocol rapidly. Only one other student needs suggestions about how to get through the day, because he had forgotten his lunch and was worried about it. The class solved the problem without the need of the teacher's assistance and appeared to be proud of this accomplishment. *__Elapsed time 18 minutes__*

8:18—The teacher again welcomes everyone to another day of school and makes a statement about a few of the important, fun, and challenging activities they will experience throughout the day. *This promotes clarity with regard to what students will be doing and learning about during the day, as well as anticipation and motivation for the learning ahead.*

WHAT ARE SOME OF THE THINGS THE TEACHER DID THAT EXEMPLIFIED AN UNDERSTANDING ABOUT HOW EMOTIONS IMPACT LEARNING?

- Taught routines and procedures to students that enhance their comfort level so that anxiety is kept at a minimum.

- Provided a classroom environment that includes careful attention to the aesthetics, including natural light, the view of the outdoors, colorful cheerful visuals, and neat, organized areas that fostered students' abilities to be self-reliant.

- Provided a place for each child to highlight work they wanted to share with a broader audience, which promotes relevance.

- Kept her finger on the pulse of students who might need a little extra emotional support due to outside circumstances (the student whose grandmother had just died).

- Modeled language that encouraged students to express their own emotions and showed students she listened to and understood their concerns.

- Taught a protocol that encouraged students to help each other express themselves and deal with emotionally challenging situations in a healthy way.

- Provided an outlet for students to express concerns that might get in the way of their learning.

- Promoted student engagement by beginning their learning with a clear, motivating message about the relevance of what they will learn.

IDEAS FOR TEACHERS TO INCREASE EQ IN THEIR CLASSROOM

Class Meetings

When students are given the opportunity to model, practice, and solve problems using an effective protocol, the emotional climate of a classroom can benefit tremendously. *Positive Discipline in the Classroom*, a book by Nelson, Lott, and Glenn (2000) includes a complete explanation to set up effective class meetings in the classroom or school.

Class meetings can provide a tremendously healthy outlet in which to learn the language of healthy emotions; practice using this language in a real-world, relevant setting; and engaging in problem solving with peers and other caring adults who can provide models and feedback for dealing with emotions in a positive way.

The word discipline means to teach. Currently a lot of discipline in schools doesn't teach; it is reactive instead of proactive. By using some of the strategies and methods this chapter presents, all members of a school could decrease wasted time, increase productive emotions, and teach more effectively, all in one fell swoop.

Teaching Students About Their Brains

Our students are naturally drawn to learning about their brains. They understand this organ's importance and can't help but be fascinated by its miraculous functions. Teaching students about how emotions work can help them understand why they react and respond in surprising ways at times. It unveils the mysterious so students can examine responses with increased reason and insight. By understanding how emotions impact learning, students are able to see how critical their environment is to their emotions and their success, as well as the important part they play in their peers' emotions and success.

Sam's Circles

After attending a presentation about the brain and emotion at a staff meeting, Sam Sager, a teacher at Serrano Middle School in Montclair, California, wanted students to understand how their moods can shift from negative to positive, or the opposite, and that they have some control of this. After delivering a few lessons on how emotions impact learning, Sam introduced the circles. He took two cardstock circles, one red and one green, and glued them back to back. This created a disk about the size of a lemon that was green on one side and red on the other. These circles resided on the corners of his students' desks.

The purpose of the circles was to encourage students' reflection about their emotional states. If they felt more negative than positive, they placed the circle red side up; if they felt more positive than negative, they placed the circle green side up. Soon after beginning this "study," students asked Sam if they could turn their circle over if they felt their mood or state change, and he told them they could. Students quickly discovered aspects of their own emotional regulation as well as the impact their teacher had on their emotions. One thing students realized was this: Their circles could go from red to green with relatively little action. An acknowledgement, a right answer, or a think, pair, share activity might result in a positive state change. Sam facilitated discussions with regard to this experiment, encouraging the use of language that enabled students to construct their own meaning, understanding, and relevance to the experience. Students noticed other things as well. They noticed that the teacher's mood seemed contagious, as it had an impact on their own emotional valence as well as the entire classroom. If the teacher seemed upbeat, the circles tended to move from red to green quicker. If the teacher was not his usual self, the opposite was true. Mirror neurons were at work here. This simple experiment helped Sam's students gain an understanding of the role they play in their own moods and what they could do to alleviate or remedy a stormy outlook. Here are a few other insights that came from the students:

- A bad mood doesn't have to be forever.

- My peers and teachers have an impact on my mood.

- I can recognize when my mood is helping my learning or hindering my learning.

- For the most part, my mood is my choice.

- My actions impact others' moods.

- I can recognize certain kinds of thoughts and/or actions that encourage a bad mood.

- I can recognize certain kinds of thought and/or actions that encourage a good mood.

- There are things I can do to go from a bad mood to a good one.

- There are things I can do to go from a good mood to a bad one.

- My emotional state impacts the ways in which I think.

- My emotional state impacts my proficiency at school.

CHAPTER SUMMARY

Emotions impact our ability to process, learn, and remember. When someone experiences highly negative events, areas of the brain that are in charge of critical and creative thinking shut down, resulting in survival responses. Conversely, when someone experiences a positive event, the areas of the brain that are in charge of critical and creative thinking are more accessible, potentially resulting in a greater degree of this kind of thinking.

Students may experience highly negative emotional events, depending on their own personal schema and triggers. Bullying, peer relationships, and at times, teacher responses, can become triggers for students' negative emotions. It is imperative for educational leaders to eradicate events like these from schools. The thinking that negative events bring is in direct opposition to the thinking we strive for in classrooms and schools.

There are observable elements of healthy emotional valences in classrooms. Relationships, language, and classroom climate are three areas in which these valences can be witnessed, and there are methods teachers can employ to encourage positive results in each. Some of the observable characteristics of these elements include how students speak to one another, the use of positive presuppositions, the modeling of mutual respect, and a pleasant, enriched classroom climate.

The instructional leader's knowledge of how emotions impact learning can improve communication, modeling, and the ability to serve as an instructional resource. Professional development on this topic can serve as a springboard for conversations that deepen staff understanding and ultimately may positively impact the culture of a school.

POSTASSESSMENT CHAPTER 2—EMOTIONS' IMPACT ON LEARNING

1. I can communicate vital information regarding emotions and learning to my teaching staff.

2. I understand how positive and negative emotional responses can impact learning.

3. I can share strategies about creating emotionally relevant learning experiences for students.

4. I can recognize a lesson that takes advantage of beneficial emotions.

5. I can help a teacher plan learning experiences that elicit positive emotions.

QUESTIONS FOR STUDY GROUP

1. Explain to a friend why considering the emotional valence in the classroom is so relevant to learning and teaching.

2. When reflecting on your class or school, consider whether there are students whose emotional center seems to be a little more sensitive than others. Why might that be?

3. What are some things you (or students) can do in a classroom or school setting that might encourage the healthiest emotional valence possible?

Table 2.1 Rubric for Principals—Measuring the Principles of How Emotions Impact Learning

Criteria	Beginning	Developing	Practicing	Exemplifying
Understanding the topic of emotions' impact on learning **Knowledge, comprehension**	Teacher has not yet acquired the foundational understanding of how emotions impact learning.	Teacher is just starting her learning about how emotions impact learning.	Teacher has an understanding of how both positive and negative emotional events impact learning.	Teacher has a thorough understanding of how positive and negative emotional events impact learning and can explain it clearly to others.
Relating and applying ideas from the topic to the classroom **Analysis, application**	Teacher cannot relate ideas or actions from his practice to ideas regarding emotions in the classroom.	Teacher can relate one idea he has learned about emotions' impact on learning to his classroom practice.	Teacher takes ideas about how to provide emotional hooks in lessons or how to enhance the emotional valence in the classroom and applies them.	Teacher takes many ideas from how emotions impact learning and consistently applies them in lessons and classroom climate, resulting in evidence of a positive valence in the classroom.
Determining which methods and strategies will best enhance emotional valence in the classroom **Application, synthesis, evaluation**	Teacher does not yet apply the methods regarding emotions that help improve classroom climate or instruction.	Teacher experiments with classroom climate or instructional strategies that enhance emotional valence in the classroom.	Teacher regularly embeds ideas about climate and instructional methods that enhance emotional valence in the classroom.	Teacher consistently and deliberately embeds effective climate and instructional methods that enhance emotional valence in the classroom.

Table 2.2   Checklist for Teachers to Help With Emotions in the Classroom

☐ I encourage students to express emotions when warranted.

☐ I teach vocabulary that assists students in expressing their emotions.

☐ I teach students protocols that guide healthy communication:
- o "I have a different idea that is somewhat related . . . ."
- o Sam's Circles
- o Class Meetings

☐ I give students some control and choice in the classroom.

☐ I use positive presuppositions when communicating with students, peers, and parents.

☐ I plan lessons that have emotional hooks.

☐ I incorporate simulations in my lessons when appropriate.

☐ I incorporate role-play in my lessons when appropriate.

☐ I have students *practice* how to respond to emotionally charged events in class meetings.

☐ I occasionally incorporate games in my lessons.

☐ I act upon the notion that each child has unique emotional patterns.

☐ I hold students accountable in consistent, respectful ways.

☐ Our classroom has a respect policy that every child knows and understands.

☐ I begin conferences or conversations with parents on a positive note.

☐ I teach students about how the brain responds to different emotions.

☐ I strive to facilitate *"aha"* moments for students in my class.

☐ We celebrate progress in small ways in my classroom.

☐ I make a positive call home in the first month of school for as many students as I can.

☐ I communicate that I hold students accountable out of care and concern for them.

☐ I have a strident bullying policy in my classroom that is followed and monitored.

☐ I don't use sarcasm in the classroom.

☐ I get to know my students' interests and plan lessons that incorporate them.

☐ I smile often in class.

☐ I express to students that I care about them and their learning.

☐ I model how to deal with emotionally charged events in a healthy way.

☐ I model how I problem solve using students as a resource.

☐ I have a discipline policy that is clear, firm, fair, and consistent.

☐ Students complete surveys that help me understand what I can do to help them the most.

☐ I have positive relationships with parents of my students.

☐ I have parents complete surveys that help me understand how well I am communicating.

☐ I plan content lessons with emotions in mind.

☐ I understand the repercussions of negative emotional events and help students deal with them as effectively as possible.

☐ I teach students methods to calm themselves:

  ○ Breathing
  ○ Visualization
  ○ Writing
  ○ Talking/Debriefing
  ○ Exercise

Table 2.3 Red Flags in a Classroom

☐ Using sarcasm

☐ Belittling comments made to students

☐ Students disrespecting teachers

☐ Students disrespecting one another

☐ Instruction consistently lacking in emotional valence

☐ Classroom management depending on catching bad behavior only

☐ Using discipline policies that don't *teach*

☐ Teacher ignoring misbehavior

☐ Students talking while the teacher is teaching

☐ Teacher not following through with students

☐ Teacher having hostile relationships with parents

☐ Teacher communicating to peers in a disrespectful manner regarding students

☐ Teacher communicating to peers in a disrespectful manner about parents of students

(Continued)

Table 2.3 (Continued)

- ☐ Teacher communicating to others in a disrespectful manner about colleagues
- ☐ Teacher gossiping in front of peers or students
- ☐ Students having very little or no choice in the classroom
- ☐ Having a messy and cluttered classroom
- ☐ Teaching using primarily negative language
- ☐ Accenting negative behaviors instead of positive ones
- ☐ Teacher avoiding collaboration with others
- ☐ Using negative presuppositions in language
- ☐ Teacher modeling impatience or hostility when dealing with frustrating events
- ☐ Discipline policy changing depending on student or mood of teacher
- ☐ Making no attempt to get student input for classroom procedures, learning, or events
- ☐ Consistently distracting noise level in the classroom for many students
- ☐ Not seeing problems of students on other parts of the campus as applicable to classroom communication
- ☐ Having no protocol for solving problems together in the classroom

Table 2.4　Using Language to Enhance Emotions—Strategies to Use With Self, Peers, or Students

- Record yourself in class to later analyze your language and speech patterns.
- Ask an observer to note words or phrases they hear you say often in the classroom.
- Post words, phrases, or open-ended questions in places in your classroom as visual reminders of helpful language to use for student learning.
- Give yourself time to think before speaking.
- Take a deep breath before speaking.
- With your grade-level or content team, decide which word or phrase you may want to retire or add to your lexicon.
- Practice positive presuppositions in your communication.
- Practice asking clarifying questions if information is unclear.

- Practice giving sincere compliments or messages of gratitude.
- Use precise, accurate language, in as few words as possible when redirecting behavior.
- Name positive attributes or behaviors of students. Accentuate the positive.
- Have students practice giving sincere compliments or messages of gratitude.

Teacher Strategies to Use With Students

Teach students words that might be helpful when expressing emotions. These might differ depending on the developmental range and contexts of students. Some examples are listed here:

Primary	Secondary
hurt	isolated
scared	intolerant
sad	frustrated
thankful	gratitude
grateful	nervous
sad	jealous
happy	concerned
excited	envious
angry	empathy
worried	thrilled
bad	abandoned
calm	apprehensive
brave	relaxed
daring	curious

Table 2.5 Using Open-Ended Questions With Students

The use of open-ended questions with students helps elicit positive emotions in several different ways. In one way, asking an open-ended question assumes a student has the capacity to come up with an answer. In another way, these kinds of questions draw out more creative thinking in students. Some samples of open-ended stems follow:

- Tell me a little more about . . . .
- What are your thoughts about . . . ?
- What are some of the things you notice about . . . ?
- How might we have . . . ?
- Why do you think . . . ?
- When might we . . . ?
- What are some of your options . . . ?
- If you were . . . , how might you . . . ?

Table 2.6   Resources for Learning More About Emotions' Role in Learning

Books for adults:

Molecules of Emotion—Candace Pert (1997)

Synaptic Self—Joseph LeDoux (2002)

Looking For Spinoza—Antonio Damasio (2003)

Why Zebras Don't Get Ulcers—Robert Sapolsky (2004)

Emotions Revealed—Paul Ekman (2003)

Descartes' Error—Antonio Damasio (1994)

Resources for teachers:

Positive Discipline in the Classroom—Nelson, Lott, & Glenn (2000)

Fred Jones Tools for Teaching (2nd ed.)—Fred Jones (2007)

Websites on emotion:

http://www.paulekman.com/

http://psyphz.psych.wisc.edu/

http://www.unh.edu/emotional_intelligence/

Resources for students regarding emotions:

When I Feel Angry—Spelman (2000)

When I Feel Sad—Spelman (2002a)

When I Feel Scared— Spelman (2002b)

The Feelings Book: The Care and Keeping of Your Emotions—Madison (2002)

Lots of Feelings—Rotner (2003)

http://www.do2learn.com/activities/SocialSkills/EmotionAnd ScenarioCards/EmotionAndScenarioCards.html

CHAPTER 3

Attention and Engagement

My experience is what I agree to attend to.

—William James (1890, p. 403)

HOW DOES UNDERSTANDING ATTENTION AND ENGAGEMENT HELP AN INSTRUCTIONAL LEADER?

Instructional leaders that understand how and why people pay attention and engage in work can assist their staff to understand and implement methods, strategies, and curriculum design that grabs student attention and holds onto it. It is not evolutionarily reasonable to expect attention and engagement in unworthy tasks. That is not how our species has survived. There *are* things our species *is* hardwired to pay attention to—things worthy of engagement—and we can engineer the environment in classrooms and staffrooms to take advantage of these things. This chapter defines attention and engagement, clarifies the attributes of attention-getting methods and engaging work, and finally shares things the instructional leader can look for in classrooms and staffrooms that encourage attention and engagement.

Have you ever . . .

- *Looked like you were paying attention in a meeting but you were really making a mental list for your weekend fishing trip?*
- *Been so engaged in work that you lost track of time?*

INATTENTION SUBTERFUGE

Have you ever been in a meeting where your attention was expected but never arrived? You might have appeared to attend (eyes on the speaker, nodding at the appropriate times), but you may really have been mentally preparing a grocery list or preparing for your upcoming fishing trip.

Now think about what must be happening with students in some classrooms. How can teachers really tell if kids are attending? Short of an fMRI, teachers can't know for sure, but there are methods they can employ to help foster student attention as well as engagement. These are discussed later in the chapter.

FLOW

Have you ever been so engrossed in an activity that you lost track of time? This occurs when people are doing something they love to do, that has deep meaning or a sense of purpose, that delivers a sense of mastery and creativity and has a high challenge and low threat.

For example, the fluid problem solving of some artistic endeavors can elicit this kind of engagement. One might lose track of time reading a good book or brainstorming ideas for a presentation. Mihaly Csikszentmihalyi, the author of the book, *Flow* (1990), describes these optimal experiences as being in a "state of flow."

It was Einstein who said, "Put your hand on a hot stove for a minute, and it seems like an hour. Sit with a pretty girl for an hour, and it seems like a minute. THAT'S relativity." We have the potential to have schools filled with students who are experiencing the profound satisfaction that comes with flow.

ATTENTION VERSUS ENGAGEMENT

Attention *and* engagement are necessary to gain and sustain the enduring thinking and learning that is needed in classrooms. This section defines and clarifies both terms for the instructional leaders in order to equip them with the knowledge to discern the difference. There is an important distinction between attention and engagement. When adults at a school have a deep understanding of attention and engagement, they can create environments that allow students to gain and sustain focus and effort.

ATTENTION AND ENGAGEMENT SIMILARITIES

Attention and engagement are both required for substantial learning in a school setting. Both can be engineered by the teacher in the classroom. A teacher can plan and embed practices that heighten or dampen either, so in a way, a teacher has some control over student attention and engagement. In another way, both are ultimately controlled by the student, as each individual brain has the final word in that which it will attend. Lastly, both attention and engagement can be fairly elusive during an observation. Students can easily *look* like they are attending or engaged. This is one reason it is helpful for instructional leaders to dig deeper than visual observation and engage in brief conversations with students. Their responses offer answers as to whether they are truly engaged or simply playing possum.

ATTENTION

Attention is a short-term, survival-dependent response. We attend to things in order to survive. This is why an unusual noise in the classroom is a handy attention-getting tool. We are hardwired to attend to unusual, or novel, stimuli for survival. This is one way a classroom teacher has overt control over the immediate, attention-getting environment. The environment can be manipulated to orient student attention in multiple ways. Using multimodal methods such as visual cues (turning off lights), auditory cues (an unusual sound), or kinesthetic cues (raising a hand) are a few ways a teacher can gain student attention. Stimuli delivered with greater intensity usually results in greater immediate attention due to the roots of survival. Knowing this, attention can be gained by manipulating the environment and embedding cues that are novel (unexpected) and vary in intensity (soft whistle to louder clap). In terms of holding students' attention during direct-instruction or lecture, a general rule of thumb for adults is after about 10 minutes of focused attention, the brain needs a short break. That break can come in the form of a brief story; a think, pair, share activity; or a minute to write down thoughts (as long as they all somehow still relate to the current learning).

Other cues include things like using music (both novel and able to manipulate intensity with volume); using random methods to call on students (students never know who is going to be called on next); using sign language to indicate different messages (novel); turning lights on and off (intensity of stimuli); using jokes, cartoons, or other sources of humor; and putting two opposing ideas together (cognitive dissonance); these are the kinds of methods that serve to capture students' attention. However, getting student attention is just the first step in an important process.

ENGAGEMENT

After gaining a student's attention, the need for sustained attention, or engagement, comes into play. One of the most obvious ways that engagement differs from attention is that engagement refers to a longer, more protracted ability to focus and apply effort (either cognitive or physical) to an activity or thought. In general, human beings were not designed to commit sustained attention to things that we find (a) boring, (b) irrelevant, (c) difficult (without some good payoff) (d), lacking (no mental framework to attach it to), or (e) unnecessary for our survival (Medina, 2008). Another way engagement differs from attention is that engagement springs from a more obvious student-centered, intrinsic decision, as opposed to the almost involuntary decisions an attention-getting device prompts. To plan for engagement, a teacher can first use the filters of meaning, emotion, and relevance. When teachers know their students and their interests, they can better plan for engagement.

ADD/ADHD AND ATTENTION

Why is it that some people have attentional deficits? Is this acquired or is this something that people are hardwired for? Attention deficit disorder (ADD), along with attention deficit/hyperactivity disorder (ADHD) are biologically based issues that have to do with how a person's brain works. Symptoms of a student with ADD are extreme disorganization and lackadaisical or sluggish behavior. If the H is added, which stands for hyperactivity, then the student is extraordinarily active. These students are often those in classrooms blurting out instead of raising their hands or saying things that might offend a potential friend.

Some may view ADD and ADHD as learned behaviors, or choices, but in reality, an accurate diagnosis of ADD means this is not a behavioral choice but a neurological issue.

The frontal lobes act as the executive over the rest of the brain. The prefrontal cortex, part of the frontal lobes, is the area that helps people think things through, analyze, and put the brakes on impulsive or potentially damaging thoughts or behaviors. The prefrontal cortex also acts as a mediator during working memory, helping to keep information stable so that we can hold on to information that helps us learn and analyze.

A student that suffers from ADD or ADHD has an attentional system that is not working optimally. Instead of the bossy prefrontal cortex heading trouble off at the pass, dealing with impulsivity and assisting with working memory, the pathway between parts of the brain that talk to one another is not as robust in people with ADHD. This impaired pathway impacts behavior. Instead of thinking about how a rude comment might impact a peer, a student with ADHD may blurt whatever pops into his head, offending a potential friend. This is because part of the job of the prefrontal cortex is to enable a person to delay gratification and put the brakes on this kind of behavior, so when the pathway between emotional centers and the prefrontal cortex is in a weakened state, blurting seems to be the natural and accessible response.

The student with ADD *can* pay attention when engaged with something *highly* stimulating, like a video game. Video games are exciting—oftentimes the player is given a role to play in a thrilling simulation. Feedback is immediate and at times, the player may be playing under a "life or death" circumstance (in some video games, you lose a life or may actually die). The truth is, students with ADD or ADHD have *variable* attention (Ratey, 2008).

Furthermore, students with ADD or ADHD have a faulty working memory. Knowing these students have problems with their prefrontal cortex communicating with other parts of the brain helps us understand why, at times, a student with ADD or ADHD can seem incredibly forgetful. It is not uncommon for these students to be involved in the middle of a math problem and forget where they are or which step comes next or to lose their place while reading a passage. This can be incredibly frustrating for both student and teacher. But there are some environmental things we can do to help support an attention deficit. Although many suggestions that work with all students will help hold the attention of a student with ADD or ADHD, there are a few that have been researched that have proven to be quite effective (Ratey, 2008).

These include using proximity, keeping regular eye contact with students, and offering feedback frequently (especially positive, clear, and direct feedback). Other ideas include using reward systems and breaking tasks into doable subtasks. Because students with ADD or ADHD may have problems delaying gratification, a long-term reward (like getting a good grade) is not going to be as accessible to most students with ADHD as it may be to a student without.

ATTRIBUTES OF ENGAGING WORK

Some qualities of engaging work include the following:

- Personal response
- Clear models
- Emotional safety
- Intellectual safety
- Learning with others
- Feedback
- Sense of audience (purpose)
- Choice
- Variety

- Authenticity

- Rigor

- Meaning and relevance

- Sense of competency and mastery

- Familiarity

Many of these items are derived from the work of Phillip Schlechty, author of *Working on the Work* (2002). Educational consultant John Antonetti built upon Schlechty's work and provides rich, detailed information about engagement in his book, *Writing as a Measure and Model of Thinking* (2007), as well as wonderful staff development on the topic.

The items on this list probably look familiar to you as things that could easily elicit student attention. That speaks to the close relationship between attention and engagement. Note that each of these qualities are as true for classroom learning as they are for graduate level or staff development learning. Instructional leaders who understand how to engage students can serve as important instructional resources as well as role models when presenting to their own staff. This section provides a definition of each method and contextualizes each through a classroom example and then a staffroom example.

PERSONAL RESPONSE

When people are given the opportunity to respond personally, it's engaging because it enables them to use their own neural networks (schema) to respond in a way that makes sense for them (see Chapter 4). Personal responses give students a chance to share their perspective with the world and help teachers understand their students better. Getting to know learners enhances just about every aspect of teaching. Personal responses feed the hardwired need for human beings to work with and connect to other people.

Personal Response in the Classroom

To elicit rich personal responses from students, teachers should become adept at crafting questions that require students to tap into their schema or clarify their understanding of a concept. For instance, a personal response in math might be, "Out of these four shapes, which do you think is the most unfriendly and why?" (adding the unfriendly part provides cognitive dissonance, which works well to gain attention). A prompt that asks students to evaluate something and explain their opinion might also work well. For instance, "After studying inventions made during the industrial revolution, which do you think was the most critical and why?" This method opens up possibilities for student responses while assuming positive presuppositions that student have their own understanding that might be unique.

Personal Response in the Staffroom

You might use a personal response prompt to begin a year-long process of revising report cards such as, "What are your hopes and fears as we move through the process of . . . ." Vital information can be gained from teachers when provided the opportunity to share their personal response. Pitfalls or barriers can be uncovered by crafting such questions. If a staff meeting is going to involve potentially divisive information, you might want to provide a reminder to the staff of their commitment to their work with a question crafted to uncover that commitment. Everyone appreciates being given the opportunity to express their thoughts, and a personal response can provide a way to teach and learn from others.

CLEAR MODELS

Clear models mean having something that people can see, hear, or touch that represents what is expected of them. Our brains are pattern finders and seekers, so making clear models available allows us to develop patterns of what exemplary looks, sounds, and maybe feels like. Providing clear models allows us to enrich our neural networks and provides feedback to serve as verification that we are on the right track (or not).

Clear Models in the Classroom

In classrooms, clear models might come in the form of exemplary anchor papers for essays in a seventh-grade language arts classroom, a photo of what a clean block area looks like in a kindergarten classroom, or a sample hypothesis from a third-grade science notebook. Clear models provide students (and teachers) with a great deal of information in order to be able to communicate quickly, from the quality of language in an essay, to the visual clues of a clean block area, to the specific words and format in a science notebook.

Providing clear models helps students engage in various kinds of work, and models are especially helpful in teaching writing. When models of effective writing are available for students to examine, ask questions about, and compare to their own, it helps them understand what good writing is, and the feedback it provides motivates. Just as looking at a picture of a completed puzzle helps us in putting the pieces together, a clear model provides help for students, which in turn, spurs motivation that can eradicate apathy.

Clear Models in the Staffroom

In a staffroom, clear models could take the form of having sample lesson plans that include an innovation the teacher is trying at school. It could be a video of a teacher using a strategy with English learners that has proven to be effective. It could be a presentation by a teacher informing her peers about an effective assessment her students completed. Clear models can serve as anchors for teachers' collective understanding of good work.

EMOTIONAL SAFETY

Emotional Safety in the Classroom

An emotionally safe school is one where social skills are taught from kindergarten on up, where students learn and understand principles of emotional safety and how they manifest in their world. It is a place where children understand words have power to uplift or destroy. A clear, comprehensive policy on bullying exists and everyone enjoys respect. Children in schools like this are given the opportunity to verbalize problems and get help from their teacher and peers to solve it, or they become problem solvers themselves. Using class meetings, students gain skills and knowledge to become emotionally intelligent problem solvers. Classrooms that exhibit emotional safety include high functioning cooperative groups, the use of active listening and caring word choices, an absence of sarcasm, and generally happy kids (and teacher). Students who don't feel emotionally safe in a classroom will rarely, if ever, be able to engage in work at the level described by Mihaly Csikszentmihalyi in *Flow* (1990).

Emotional Safety in the Staffroom

To engender emotional safety in a staffroom, one of the most profound things a leader can do is model emotional intelligence. This means seeking to understand behavior that derails a meeting or language that diminishes respect among colleagues. It means having uncomfortable conversations with careful facilitation of the emotional valence in the room. It means crafting, clarifying, and committing to a respect policy among the staff that is meaningful and relevant, and then clarifying some more. Instructional leaders *must* walk the talk in terms of emotional intelligence and safety. They need to address unsafe practices in a consistent, effective, sensitive manner. They need to ensure that everyone understands it is unequivocally unacceptable to bully, insult, or disrespect others. Aside from helping create an engaging work environment, this is a prerequisite to building the kind of trust that is so beneficial for leaders to engender.

INTELLECTUAL SAFETY

The idea of intellectual safety goes hand in hand with emotional safety. Intellectual safety includes ideas that enjoy replication in some of the most successful, innovative organizations in the world, such as the ability to foster divergent thinking, suspend judgment, and live with ambiguity. Intellectual safety understands that there will be phases to our understanding, and we can't always be all-knowing. It understands that people might leave a meeting having to delve deeper into a problem, or do a little research of their own, or ask more questions.

Intellectual Safety in the Classroom

One of the best ways to foster intellectual safety in the classroom is through teacher modeling. The teacher can model what someone who is suspending judgment does, how thinking divergently sounds, or what tolerating ambiguity is like. The teacher can also be the lookout to find others in the classroom following suit. Pointing out this ability and clarifying to all when it occurs will help students understand what is meant by intellectual safety. This is the teacher who allows the boy who has a penchant for gardening to create a raised bed garden on the counter and encourages experimentation while controlling for variables such as sunlight, water, and so forth. Or this is the teacher who encourages the girl who is fascinated by the Hopi to create a recipe book of their diet. Intellectual safety is an imperative quality in order to build a nation filled with students who have the skills necessary to succeed in the 21st century.

Intellectual Safety in the Staffroom

Again, the best way to foster intellectual safety for teachers is by modeling it as the instructional leader. Counterintuitive as it might sound, sometimes the quality of intellectual safety is modeled through instructional leaders being able to admit they don't have the answer(s), or they aren't certain about which decision is the best. That's the first step. The second step for instructional leaders would be to allow their inability to have the answers serve as a starting point for their own inquiry. Intellectual safety in a staffroom is not just a helpful element for engaging work; it is a prerequisite.

LEARNING WITH OTHERS

Learning with others meets our hardwired need to be included in a tribe and to work with and help others. It helps engage us for these evolutionarily evident reasons and more. Learning with others often includes a natural source of feedback. We gain ideas and understanding from others. It adds a human connection and feedback and increases resources, and for some of us, it's just more fun—all things that stimulate engagement.

Learning With Others in the Classroom

Cooperative learning structures, like using peer coaches, is one way learning with others may manifest in a classroom. I saw a brilliant use of learning with others in a classroom a few weeks ago when the students became "coaches" after showing their mastery of a concept. Teachers can create learning teams in classrooms where partners or trios are given a topic to research or a task that can result in engagement skyrocketing. The only caveat to this structure is the child that is an extreme introvert. In these cases, the teacher needs to be sensitive to the child's needs and pair her with the most appropriate choice of peer.

Learning With Others in the Staffroom

Learning with others in a staffroom can be as simple and informal as teachers stopping into each others' classrooms before or after school to question their colleagues regarding structured grade-level teams, content teams, PLCs, action research, leadership teams, and so forth. Some of the highest functioning teachers are the ones that are (a) highly engaged, (b) experiencing the most success, and (c) often the most pleasant to be around, which could be a function of their emotional and intellectual safety. Encouraging learning with others can be fostered by deliberately using methods that require others in learning. These can include simple methods during a staff meeting such as think, pair, share activities or more complex methods such as inquiry-based action research completed by teams. Taking advantage of our natural inclination to learn with others can motivate and propel teachers in their professional development and cultivate a climate of continuous learning.

FEEDBACK

The next chapter goes into more depth about feedback, but because it is such a powerful element, it won't hurt to see the connections it has to heightening engagement. When people are learning, the brain is making connections, strengthening current neural networks, or even forging new ones. We are integrating information, forming hypotheses, and actively testing. Feedback helps motivate learners to continue, and in doing so, helps the entire learning cycle.

Feedback in the Classroom

In the classroom, feedback can flow from teacher to students and vice versa. Teachers who get feedback from their students on things like classroom climate and instruction gain an edge over those who do not. It can be a huge help in building an effective student-centered program. Another effective (and more common) form of feedback occurs when teachers give feedback to students. The purpose of the feedback can vary, from helping students see progress to guiding students to find strengths or weaknesses in their work. Feedback informs learners of where they are on the path to success, and it outlines the steps necessary to stay on a beneficial trajectory. Feedback from students to teachers can be in the form of surveys, Quick Writes, or journal entries. Feedback from teachers to students can take the form of written comments, conversations, conferences, (both in class and after school with parents) grades, quizzes, and exit cards.

Feedback in the Staffroom

Instructional leaders can provide feedback to staff through notes, walk-through forms, checklists, conversation, and surveys. Instructional leaders can use surveys that teachers or parents complete regarding matters at school as feedback, which can provide a more complete understanding of the best path to take in different matters, much like notes from an observation help teachers understand the best path to take to improve their practice.

SENSE OF AUDIENCE

When our work includes a clear sense of audience, a greater sense of purpose may form. This concept draws from our innate desire to learn with and help others. A sense of audience generates meaning and emotion that are catalysts for significant processing and learning

Sense of Audience in the Classroom

Students who experience a rich sense of audience often have a classroom that extends far beyond the classroom walls, such as classrooms where children's work is meaningful and connected to people "on the outside," where students participate in field trips in the community or have pen pals in other places. A sense of audience can be increased by collecting student narratives, binding them, and creating a classroom book for the library. This quality flourishes when an actual audience exits, whether that takes the form of a play, performance, or at a student-led conference. It acts as a conduit for engagement, and it includes a great reason to practice, rehearse, edit, and ensure accuracy in student work. In fact, students with a clear sense of audience are often the ones reminding the teacher of the need for practice instead of the other way around.

Sense of Audience in the Staffroom

A staff that has a sense of audience understands the connection between their work and the greater community. They are aware of the needs they fulfill in their students and how their work impacts the greater community. A sense of audience for teachers can occur when they share their work with others. This might take place during a team meeting, PLC time, or a leadership opportunity. Presenting during professional development opportunities or outside conferences is another way a sense of audience appears. Some of my most engaging moments as an educator have been spent in the service of others, with a clear sense of audience.

CHOICE

When people are able to make choices about how to approach a task, what kind of task they will do, and who they will work with, engagement is heighted. Think of how disappointing it would be to not be given a choice next time you went to buy something. When choice is limited (or removed), the emotional valence can lose its optimistic light and engagement can dissolve.

Choice in the Classroom

Students who are given choices at school will more likely stay engaged in their work. A healthy balance must be struck to optimize learning. Perhaps students get to make some decisions about their learning each day. Maybe they get a menu of work to choose from to complete during the day, or they get to choose topics they will research, or they get to choose their partner during cooperative work, or they have a voice in designing the school's bullying policy. Some choice will increase engagement, efficacy, and motivation for students. It may serve the school to listen carefully to the voices of students, as students may come up with brilliant ways to solve even adult-sized problems.

Choice in the Staffroom

Instructional leaders need to be able to trust teachers and teachers need to be worthy of trust for choice to flourish at a school site. An example in classrooms where choice was impacted was seen with some of the reading-first protocols implemented in schools in the past decade. It included mandatory elements that impacted choice for teachers. Scenarios ranged from exceedingly prescriptive, to somewhat prescriptive, and schools where choice became scarce suffered. Many masterful teachers felt like their autonomy was stripped away. They felt a loss of security and efficacy, and teacher unhappiness resulted. These are the professionals who had devoted their lives to teaching—being told that a publishing conglomerate knew the needs of the students better than they did. You can see why removing choice can have devastating results.

VARIETY

When too many elements of our lives become habituated, we can become entrenched in ways of doing, acting, and knowing that spring from comfort as opposed to innovation or critical thinking. Variety acts to combat unhealthy habituation in classrooms and staffrooms alike.

Variety in the Classroom

A teacher can provide variety in content (what students learn), process (how they learn it), and product (how they show they learned it). Teachers can also use a variety of instructional strategies, processing strategies, and assessment strategies in the classroom. Variety can be used in the setup of the classroom, adding or editing things, moving things around, or even changing students' seats. If teachers are ever looking for an antidote for boredom, they should try variety and see what happens to the engagement of the group.

Variety in the Staffroom

Variety triggers the arousal system in our brains. This is why, if every staff meeting includes a habituated structure, the instructional leader might consider changing how the information is delivered. Instead of the usual structure of teachers collaborating in grade-level teams, perhaps they are grouped differently. Instead of going through all the points that were brought up by a team in a lecture format, perhaps the big ideas are written on chart paper and groups rotate around, read them, and add their input. Variety helps to stimulate our thinking and gets our creative juices flowing, and when these things are occurring, engagement is more likely.

AUTHENTICITY

Authentic work is real and meaningful. One of the filters the brain uses is meaning. If something is meaningful, there is a better chance processing and memory will be more effective.

Authenticity in the Classroom

In the classroom, authenticity can be found when students are given time to move through a process with differentiation. Real writers don't complete a piece in 45 minutes, mathematicians don't sit in isolation practicing problem after problem, and scientists don't read textbooks punctuated by the occasional lab. Writers understand and use a process to go from thought to written articulation, mathematicians talk with colleagues and solve proofs, and scientists form hypotheses, collect data, and write, write, write. Students who are routinely given forms to fill out, or random graphic organizers to complete a piece of writing, or who complete algorithm after algorithm in isolation, or read about the world of science instead of experiencing it, are not engaged in authentic practice. I once watched as a group of seventh graders from Brad Cuff's history class in Mt. Baldy, California, create a "dig" for third and fourth graders after creating their own civilization, complete with an economy, a political system, religion, and so forth. Engagement throughout this process was off the charts. They were asking to stay in from recess and lunch to work. This is the kind of authentic work that can be embedded and increases engagement.

Authenticity in the Staffroom

Action research and sharing information through blogs or articles can promote authenticity with teachers. Authentic meetings result in a plan of action that makes a difference in the life of a student. Lesson plans are works of authenticity because they are how our profession codifies phases of instruction and learning. This is probably one reason why the best lesson plans are those that are tailored for a class, where the teacher can add, edit, or create new or unique components. Part of the reason people sneer at paperwork is because it feels inauthentic. Authentic work is work in which we sustain engagement.

RIGOR

Our brains are pattern-seeking problem solvers. When we encounter rigorous events, engagement often results. When rigor couples with intellectual safety, it further expands engagement. There is an example of this in the movie *Apollo 13*. In the scene, ground control has discovered that the men in the spaceship lack the proper fitting for the hose that delivers adequate oxygen to their craft. They gather their best minds, bring in a box of miscellaneous parts available to the men on the craft, dump it on the table and say, "Gentlemen, we have to find a way to fit a round peg in a square hole." At once the team digs in and ultimately finds a way to save the day. Although all our problems are not life or death, as this one was, the rigor that comes with complex problems adds a level of engagement, especially when people have some sense of mastery, enough resources, and a deadline.

Rigor in the Classroom

A classroom that includes rigorous work is a classroom where the teacher has high expectations of his students and trusts that students have the capacity to solve rigorous problems. The teacher needs to equip students to deal with the kinds of thinking that rigorous work requires. Rigor in the classroom might take the form of a problem of the day, or embedded high-level questions in lessons throughout the day. Rigor might come in the form of the process, the product, or the content. For students to engage in rigorous work, portions of the curriculum and daily activities need to be aligned with the upper levels of Bloom's Taxonomy. The instructional leader should witness these upper levels of Bloom's Taxonomy in components of what students are expected to do on a daily basis.

Rigor in the Staffroom

Having structures available for problem solving can help the instructional leader guide individuals, teams, and whole groups of teachers in rigorous work. These structures might include having teachers (a) clearly define and describe the problem presented, (b) think about different ways they have dealt with similar problems in the past, (c) brainstorm different possible solutions, (d) advocate for solutions that make sense, (e) identify steps or resources needed to solve the problem, (f) identify indicators of success (how they will know they are making progress or the problem is solved), and (g) make commitments to parts people may play in solving the problem. Protocols can guide individuals or groups through rigorous problem-solving events with scaffolding that can make rigor feel stimulating as opposed to unfeasible.

SENSE OF COMPETENCE

A sense of competence helps us persevere during challenging physical or cognitive events. Competence gives us the edge we need to interpret a task as manageable, as opposed to unfeasible. When we experience competence, our brains are bathing in neurotransmitters that enhance reward and pleasure. In this way, success begets success.

Sense of Competence in the Classroom

How many of us have seen the student in the classroom that has given up, whose default position includes apathy and learned helplessness? Responses like these are the *opposite* of engagement and can result from feeling incompetent. A teacher that nurtures competence operates, at times, from students' strengths. These teachers determine what students *can* do, and they build skills and knowledge from there. Learning progressions (which are described in detail in Chapter 5) are a tool that helps students build skills to incrementally gain a sense of competence. It can be especially helpful for struggling students.

Sense of Competence in the Staffroom

A teacher shows a sense of competence when his response to a problem is one of measured thoughtfulness. This teacher has a degree of efficacy that helps keeps him in a state of mind required for critical thinking. He is a teacher with a growth mindset and a deep belief that answers will come, problems will be solved, and situations will improve, through effort and competency. The instructional leader who keeps his finger on the pulse of his staff's level of knowledge, competence, and mastery of critical features of their work is going to be able to support those that need to build their competency.

MEANING AND RELEVANCE

What we find meaningful and relevant we process more efficiently, we remember more readily, and we are much more apt to become engaged by.

Meaning and Relevance in the Classroom

Classrooms that include meaningful work are often classrooms that enjoy high engagement, energy, and curiosity. These are behaviors and characteristics that are needed in 21st-century learners. Meaningful, relevant work in classrooms is work that is linked to students and their community. This kind of work is done when students complete research regarding the quality of their community's water, write a book with stories of people who improve the quality of life in their community, or train for a local 5k run in physical education. Although the meaning and relevance might wax and wane depending on the content and curriculum, the intentional insertion of some of these qualities in the content, process, and products we ask of our students will serve to increase the engagement in classrooms.

Meaning and Relevance in the Staffroom

Meaningful work in staffrooms is work that has direct links with helping students or other teachers learn, and it results in knowledge and actions that improve the current situation or are worthwhile and pivotal for improving a teacher's practice. Effective PLCs can serve to enhance meaning and relevance for teachers. Examining student work and designing effective assessments are examples of meaningful and relevant work for teachers. The meaning in these kinds of activities springs from the valuable information teachers gain from analysis, reflection, and dialogue with colleagues. Meaningful mission statements speak to the heart of why the staff arrives at school every day for 180 days a year. Meaningful and relevant professional development is the kind of learning that causes a shift in thinking, helps teachers solve their problems, improves their practice, or ignites a desire to learn more.

CONNECTING INSTRUCTIONAL LEADER KNOWLEDGE AND SKILL SETS TO ATTENTION AND ENGAGEMENT

Resource Provider

Instructional leaders who understand the tenets of what captures and holds students' attention can assist teachers in understanding and implementing these tenets in their classroom. Providing professional development to help teachers understand the difference between attention and engagement, supporting teachers in crafting coherent, common understandings about what attention and engagement look like in classrooms, and being able to point teachers in the right direction with regard to effective resources that increase student attention or engagement, are all actions that provide critical resources for the classroom teacher.

Instructional Resource

Instructional leaders who understand attention and engagement can provide teachers with valuable feedback regarding student attention and engagement in their classroom. These informed observations can serve as a topic for reflective conversations with the teacher. The instructional leader can serve as a resource who guides teachers in planning instruction that takes advantage of these qualities. Finally, the instructional leader can use this knowledge as a filter when examining lesson plans or choosing instructional materials for future use.

Good Communicator

Instructional leaders occasionally need to communicate critical information to groups. By understanding what grabs and holds an audience's attention, the instructional leader can incorporate "hooks" that accomplish this feat. Beginning with a statement that grabs people emotionally, surprises them, makes them laugh, or helps them see how important they are in a process, and attending to issues of timing and relevance, the speaker not only captures attention but holds onto it to encourage effective processing and recall.

PROFESSIONAL DEVELOPMENT FOR ATTENTION AND ENGAGEMENT

What seems like engagement to one teacher might be disengagement to another. It is important, therefore, to define and clarify attention and engagement, which may require time at a staff meeting or professional development day to dialogue and discuss the topic as a staff.

The instructional leader can build a definition of these two concepts and what they look and sound like in a classroom (clear model). It is vitally important to clarify the difference between a fun activity that grabs attention and the work that goes into planning for engagement.

Professional development for this topic can begin with a prompt about attention (personal response), followed by a conversation about how it manifests in the classroom. A double bubble (a Thinking Map that is used for comparing and contrasting) might be completed with attention on one side and engagement on the other. I have done this in numerous presentations and it has proven to be a fruitful activity because of the opportunity it brings to provide corrective instruction for misconceptions about these concepts as well as building a collective understanding about what attention and engagement look like, sound like, and feel like in the school (clear model). Through activities such as these, an instructional leader can get at the core of misconceptions and concerns and make some tremendous progress toward goals with regard to increasing both attention and engagement at a school site (intellectual safety).

After initial staff development, the instructional leader can craft walk-through forms (using information taken from staff— authenticity) and begin to quantify and measure something as elusive as engagement. It will become less elusive, especially if teachers are given the opportunity to take part in revisions of the walk-through form to refine the contents (meaning, relevance, intellectual safety).

WHAT TO LOOK FOR IN A LESSON PLAN

A lesson plan built for attention and engagement will include qualities of engaging work and attention-getting strategies. There are books on student attention and engagement, and the Internet is replete with ways to hook learners. If teachers have access and a little training in attention and engagement, along with the information from this chapter, they could be well equipped to embed attention getters and engaging work in their lesson and unit plans.

An engaging lesson plan will include methods to gain the attention and engagement of students. Some phases of a lesson (at the beginning or right after transitions) benefit from attention getters, whereas different phases of lessons (during processing and practice) benefit from embedding qualities of engaging work. Quick, attention-getting strategies are used at the beginning of a learning cycle (there can be many learning cycles in one lesson; a decent rule of thumb is about every 10 minutes), whereas the qualities of engaging work relate more to the content of the lesson and unit and are usually embedded during the planning phase.

In the following, read how one teacher gains attention and engagement in the classroom. The wording in italics is like having a whisper coach in the classroom, making overt links to the research behind attention and engagement in the classroom. The elapsed time is bolded, italicized, and underlined.

SAMPLE OBSERVATION OF A TEACHER WHO UNDERSTANDS THE PRINCIPLE

Teacher: Third Grade

Subject and time of day: Math—1:00 PM

Learning target: Students will practice and articulate different ways to divide.

Time observed: 20 minutes

The instructional leader is in class as the students enter after lunch. Some students are visibly tired, some are quiet, and some are chatting as they enter the classroom. Although these differences in comportment are obvious, every child finds their spot in the classroom in little time. The teacher begins the lesson by saying, in a sing-song manner, "Good afternoon my friends," to which every child orients their attention to their teacher and responds in unison, "Good afternoon Ms. Cortez." *It is apparent that this has been a practiced device to gain student attention and still remains somewhat novel to students. This has effectively oriented every child's visual focus to the same spot in the classroom.* The teacher informs students what they will be accomplishing during the lesson. She ties the learning target (understanding and articulating different ways we can divide) to a big idea that the class is working on and integrates several content areas. The class has created a company that will create, market, and sell a product. The big idea that this connects to is "wants and needs." This big idea has multiple applications, from social science standards regarding economy to science standards regarding survival. After informing students of the learning target, she claps her hands together and says, "Teach" to the students. *This is another procedure that students automatically complete. Students take turns summarizing the learning target and how it is going to help them accomplish one of their goals for their company. This heightens the relevance of this learning for every student in the classroom. They are able to articulate*

(Continued)

(Continued)

not only why they are learning how to divide but how it will help them in the future. **_Elapsed time 5 minutes_**

Children are in trios (*learning with others*) and shown a word problem with images to help scaffold their understanding (*rigorous, complex problems*). It is a word problem related to their class company's product (they are packaging and selling seeds from their classroom garden's harvest last fall). Here is what is projected on the board:

We have over 345 sunflower seeds to package. We have decided to put in 10–12 seeds per package. How many packages are we going to need to create if we choose 10 seeds per package? Will that number change if we put in 12 seeds per package? How do you know this? Can you estimate how many packages we would need if we only put in 5 seeds per package?

Once again, relevance is key to the engagement seen in each small group of children. The entire class chorally reads the word problem and a random student is chosen to summarize what they need to do in order to solve the problem. *This takes advantage of a novelty and learning with others while clarifying the task.* Students are given time and resources (big pieces of paper, markers, counters, etc.) to solve the problem and share their solution with words, numbers, drawings, or tables. They understand they will be responsible for articulating to the rest of the class how they solved the problem. *These methods are taking advantage of learning with others, authenticity, rigor, and relevance.* **_Elapsed time 10 minutes_**

Students are then given time to ponder, talk, negotiate, problem solve, draw, clarify, talk some more, and ask questions of peers and the teacher. As the instructional leader walks around the room to probe a little deeper about student engagement, she asks children three questions: "What are you doing? Why are you doing this? How will it help you in the future?" As a result of her informal survey, all four children she asked these questions of answered them to her satisfaction. *This is additional evidence of engagement and relevance.* **_Elapsed time 15 minutes_**

The teacher checks in on the progress of the students. Five of the eight groups have information to share regarding their progress on the problem. One group has drawn out the problem using icons for packages and seeds. One group has begun a table with the Y axis showing the number of seeds and the X axis showing the number of packages. Another group has the algorithm shown with labels showing what the different numbers stand for. *This takes advantage of learning with others, authenticity, intellectual safety, and relevance. These elements appear to be some of the reasons that all students, whether or not they have finished their problem solving, appear to be excited, attentive, and engaged in the math lesson.* Students that are in groups ready to share are now given one minute to articulate their progress so far, while students still working have one minute to ask clarifying questions. *The degree of relevance and rigor is high as these third graders ask questions about factoring in variables like the occasional unusable seed or package.* **_Elapsed time 20 minutes_**

Although the lesson has not yet come to a close, the instructional leader needs to leave, but she feels confident in recording some of the attention-getting devices as well as engaging qualities she witnessed. Here are a few of the things she may have written down.

WHAT ARE SOME OF THE THINGS THE TEACHER DID TO TAKE ADVANTAGE OF ATTENTION AND ENGAGEMENT?

- The teacher used attention-getting devices like tone of voice, choral responses, and signals at the beginning portion of the lesson to orient student attention.

- The teacher used novelty judiciously during the lesson.

- As students begin to complete these problems, the visuals created are posted on the walls of the classroom to serve as clear models for this kind of problem solving in the future.

- The teacher ties relevant content to the students' learning target.

- The teacher prepares a rigorous problem for students to solve.

- The teacher uses whole-class participation methods (choral response, teach a partner) to increase energy, attention, and engagement at certain times during the lesson.

- The teacher embeds learning with others in multiple ways; the students are helping others by solving a problem that will benefit the entire class, helping each other in their trios as they problem solve, and helping their peers understand a mathematical skill.

- The teacher embeds authenticity in the lesson as this is the kind of thinking and activity that actually happens in the real world when organizations are faced with a problem.

- The teacher honors the unique ways students chose to solve their problems, thus embedding intellectual and emotional safety throughout the lesson.

CHAPTER SUMMARY

Although they share some common attributes, attention and engagement are two different things. Attention is more of a short-term, survival-based response that orients people to attend. A teacher can gain student attention by providing some form of stimuli that is novel, highly interesting, or different in intensity than normal. Engagement, on the other hand, refers to sustained attention and focus. If teachers tried to use the same strategies they used to gain student attention in an effort to sustain engagement, they might not enjoy much success. Engaging work includes qualities that help us to attend and continue, even in the face of adversity. Some qualities of engaging work include the following: personal response, clear models, emotional safety, intellectual safety, learning with others, feedback, sense of audience, choice, variety, authenticity, rigor, and meaning or relevance. When teachers embed these into their planning and instruction, engagement of students is more likely to rise, as evidenced by sustained effort, improved quality of work, and more involvement and participation in the classroom.

In the tables at the end of the chapter (see Tables 3.1–3.4), the instructional leader will find ideas and tools to measure the manifestation of attention and engagement in classrooms and staffrooms. Table 3.1 contains a rubric that will aid in measuring attention and engagement in the classroom. Table 3.2 shows how instruction can move from irrelevant to engaging. Table 3.3 further explains the qualities of engaging work, and Table 3.4 contains resources for teachers.

POSTASSESSMENT CHAPTER 3—ATTENTION AND ENGAGEMENT

1. I can describe the relationship between attention and engagement.

2. I can share strategies that help gain a student's attention with teachers.

3. I can share strategies that help engage a learner with teachers.

4. I can recognize attention and engagement in a classroom observation.

5. I can assist a teacher in planning with qualities of engaging work in mind.

QUESTIONS FOR STUDY GROUP

1. Where do you think your school is in terms of attention and engagement? Why do you believe this to be so?

2. Do you feel attention and engagement are mutually exclusive? Why or why not?

3. What qualities of engaging work do you see the most often? Why do you think this is so?

4. What qualities of engaging work do you see least often? Why do you think this is so?

5. Where would you begin in terms of leading a school to increase attention and engagement?

Table 3.1 Rubric for Principals—Measuring Teachers' Knowledge and Skills With Attention and Engagement

Criteria	Beginning	Developing	Practicing	Exemplifying
Understanding the topic of attention and engagement **Knowledge, comprehension**	Teacher does not yet know or understand the tenets of attention or engagement.	Teacher is just starting her learning about attention or engagement and cannot yet indicate differences between them.	Teacher can indicate the differences between attention and engagement and uses a strategy or two for both.	Teacher has a thorough understanding of attention and engagement and consistently embeds attention-getting structures and qualities of engaging work in planning and instruction.
Relating and applying ideas from the topic to the classroom **Analysis, application**	Teacher cannot yet relate ideas or actions from their practice to ideas regarding attention or engagement.	Teacher can relate one idea he has learned about attention or engagement to his practice and applies it.	Teacher takes ideas about attention and engagement and uses them at times to design effective lessons.	Teacher takes many ideas from attention and engagement and consistently applies them in lessons, resulting in increased student engagement.
Determining which methods and strategies will best enhance attention and engagement in different situations **Application, synthesis, evaluation**	Teacher does not yet apply the methods that help increase attention or engagement.	Teacher experiments with attention-getting strategies or qualities of engaging work in a limited manner, with support.	Teacher regularly embeds some kind of attention-getting strategies as well as qualities of engaging work in her instruction and planning.	Teacher consistently and deliberately embeds effective attention-getting strategies and qualities of engaging work in her instruction and planning and measures effectiveness in some way.

Table 3.2 From Irrelevant to Engaging

Irrelevant	Insert Quality of Engaging Work	Engaging
Students fill in vocabulary words in premade worksheets.	Rigor, novelty, learning with others	In pairs, students create a sentence frame that requires them to understand the vocabulary word in order to complete it (e.g., for the word "frost," the students might come up with a sentence frame such as, "You could tell there was frost on the car because _____").
Students write a paragraph summarizing their science lab results.	Learning with others, feedback	Students get into pairs and summarize their learning to each other, using a structure that allows each student the opportunity to give and get feedback, as well as learn from one another. Then they write.
Students read the textbook silently or in a round-robin manner.	Clear model, novelty	Students are given chunks of reading to practice and read through ahead of time, thereby giving them time to practice for fluency. They then read aloud using the best voice for the purpose (e.g., newscaster voice for current events, character voice for novel, narrator for historical text, etc.).
Students watch as the teacher works out math problems on the board.	Intellectual safety, learning with others, rigor	Students are given the opportunity to problem solve during math using multiple formats (drawing, using tables, etc.), working in pairs or trios and articulating their reasoning.

(Continued)

Table 3.2 (Continued)

Irrelevant	Insert Quality of Engaging Work	Engaging
Students begin a new unit of study by looking in the textbook.	Personal response, learning with others	Students are asked to think about how the big ideas or important concepts from the unit of study relate to their life in some way and then share their response with others.
Students complete a worksheet on punctuation.	Novelty, humor, learning with others, relevance	Students work in trios to create correctly punctuated sentences related to a topic in a content area and then share the sentences using sound effects for different punctuation symbols.
Students complete a worksheet (any kind) in isolation.	Learning with others, intellectual safety, clear models, feedback	Students work as a whole class team to solve each problem or group of problems. The first two or three students to complete each chunk of the task are checked for accuracy. They then become "coaches" to provide feedback to their peers as they finish the problems.
Students read about a concept in social science in their textbook.	Novelty, learning with others, relevance	Students participate in a simulation that integrates a similar concept(s) that they will be learning about in their social science unit (e.g., students have limited time to work together to make as many paper airplanes as possible without any communication or feedback to introduce the concept of the assembly line at the beginning of a unit on industrialization).

Table 3.3 Qualities of Engaging Work

Engaging Quality	Examples in a Classroom
Personal Response	This includes journals, Quick Writes, sentence-framed prompts, or anything you see in a classroom that asks students to express their own opinions or viewpoints on a topic with the intention of sharing with others.
Learning With Others	This includes anything where learners are not isolated: think, pair, share activities; learning partners; learning appointments; trios, debates, team problem solving; student "coaches"; cooperative learning structures.
Novelty	This includes the use of the unusual or novel item, image, learning structure, or topic. Examples may include incorporating movement into the learning (often this results in novelty since movement is not necessarily a regular modality for teaching or learning) or anything relevant that the class has not yet experienced.
Meaning and Relevance	This shows up in planning as well as instruction and assessment. Meaning and relevance is heightened when the learning can be tied to a broad concept that students find important and/or valuable in their world or a concept that students find particularly interesting.
Feedback	This includes anything in a classroom that helps students self-assess or come to an understanding of where they are on their trajectory in learning serving as feedback. Structures like reciprocal teaching, the use of whiteboards, and methods to help students measure progress all serve as feedback.
Emotional and Intellectual Safety	Emotional and intellectual safety in a classroom is evidenced by students who willingly take risks often, who are willing to suspend judgment, or who are able to understand and live with ambiguity in certain circumstances.
Clear Models	Both teachers and students can provide clear models in every content area for the students of the class. Clear models might take the form of exemplary work posted in a specific location in the classroom for students to access when needed or a teacher-led inspection of specific clear models before, during, or after a task students are asked to complete.
Humor	Humor can be embedded in different ways into the classroom, whether that means it is part of the natural way for students and teacher to deal with their world or it means there are certain times and ways that humor is part of the school day. Jokes, cartoons, or a lighthearted approach to aspects of the school day are all examples of humor in the classroom.
Rigor	Rigor in a classroom is most evidenced by examining what or how we ask our students to do, think, act, and produce. Evidence of rigor in an individual lesson can be captured by close attention to the level of questions and tasks asked of students. Questions and tasks that require thinking from the upper level of Bloom's Taxonomy are what rigor requires.

Table 3.4 Resources for Attention and Engagement Strategies

Books:

Writing as a Measure and Model of Thinking—John Antonetti (2007)

Working on the Work—Phillip Schlechty (2002)

Quantum Teaching—DePorter, Reardon, & Singer-Nourie (1999)

New Management Handbook—Rick Morris (1997)

Tools and Toys—Rick Morris (1995)

Cooperative Learning—Spencer Kagan (1994)

Websites: (filled with great products for attention and engagement)

http://www.kaganonline.com

http://www.newmanagement.com

http://www.smartclassroommanagement.com

CHAPTER 4

The Power of Processing

Learning should be an active process. Too often students come to school to watch their teachers work. When students use what they learn they remember the information better and understand the utility of what is being taught.

—Willard Dagget (company poster)

This chapter provides the instructional leader with key concepts related to processing, gives examples of what an instructional leader can look for as evidence of effective processing in the classroom and the staffroom, and gives you ideas about how to incorporate this topic in your work with adults at the school site. The chapter will close with resources that the instructional leader can use to support teachers with this principle.

Have you ever . . .

- *Tried to read on an airplane and found it too difficult because of too many distractions?*
- *Failed to grasp an understanding of a concept?*
- *Understood a concept almost immediately with what seemed like little effort?*

83

THE EFFECTS OF SENSORY OVERLOAD ON PROCESSING

I was on an airplane recently and attempted to read something while the crew and passengers prepared for flight. There I sat with a research article in my lap, as my eyes moved across the page. I recognized all the words, paused at the end of sentences, decoded accurately and fluently. Yet when I completed my reading, I had no idea what I had just read. Why?

This is due to processing issues. Perhaps it was because the child behind me repeatedly asked his father questions. Maybe it was the child in the back of the plane who was screaming, as if the pain of an ear infection was underway. Maybe it had to do with the flight attendant frequently breaking in over the PA system to give passengers direction. Or maybe, it was the incessant, high-pitched, whirring of the engines that hampered my processing.

I couldn't process effectively because I was experiencing sensory overload. My brain was busy consciously and unconsciously processing the hive of activity on the plane, making the processing required for the research article unfeasible.

THINGS THAT INHIBIT PROCESSING

At times you might be in an optimal learning environment but still experience trouble grasping key points of the learning. This might occur for a new principal at her first principal meeting in a new district. Picture attending a meeting where every other member has built a shared understanding about the district's revision of a new grading and reporting system. The other 25 principals in the meeting have completed and shared professional development together regarding best practices in grading and reporting, examined other district's grading and reporting systems, and completed research with regard to the most effective models of grading and reporting. This group has developed shared neural networks. Members have learned together and from one another, forming a group brain, a collective body of knowledge. After hearing some ideas this team of principals is building upon to create a cohesive grading and reporting system, you are asked to add your ideas to the conversation. Because you don't have a lot of prior knowledge about grading and reporting systems and have not participated with this group, you might be hard-pressed to effectively process the information, because you are having trouble fitting it into your own scant mental model on the topic, or, neurologically speaking, your own sparse neural networks. When current neural networks are co-opted, the pathways or mental models that you know already exist in a learner's brain; new information can be overlaid onto a known route that's already been paved. If, on the other hand, the neural networks are not extensive, as in the case just mentioned, the need for scaffolding and other kinds of support is necessary to move from novice to proficient or expert.

PROCESSING THAT
SEEMS EFFORTLESS

Within a few seconds of entering a classroom, some instructional leaders glean essential information about instruction and student understanding that can provide valuable feedback for the classroom teacher. Their processing of the environment and events is rapid and accurate. A few things help this occur. One has to do with the instructional leader's confidence and competence in observation skills. Another has to do with the knowledge the instructional leader possesses regarding what to look for in classrooms that provides evidence for effective instruction and learning. There are many ways instructional leaders can gain, maintain, and continually add to their knowledge and skills in this arena. One might be through engaging in walk-throughs followed by thoughtful dialogue with colleagues regarding the next level of work for the team. Another is through the continual research and learning that an instructional leader makes a priority. Lastly, instructional leaders can gain, maintain, and continually add to their repertoire when they *consistently spend time examining, analyzing, and reflecting upon instruction in classrooms.* The following section provides instructional leaders with information from the world of neuroscience and cognitive science that will help them understand why processing is such a critical component for learners.

TWO FILTERS TO CONSIDER— RELEVANCE AND ENVIRONMENT

Processing is the act of taking in information with the intent to learn, use, and recall it. Before we get into the biology behind processing, we must address two filters that effect processing: relevance and environment.

When the content is something that is highly relevant to the learner, chances are processing will be heightened or enhanced (or made easier) for the learner (Caine et al., 2009; Willingham, 2009; Wolfe, 2010). If the environment maintains a valence of high interest and low threat, processing will be enhanced as well. These two elements are represented in the following graph. If both of these elements fall in the upper right quadrant of the graph, it's a fair bet that the learner will process the information with more fervor and motivation, thereby effecting processing effectiveness.

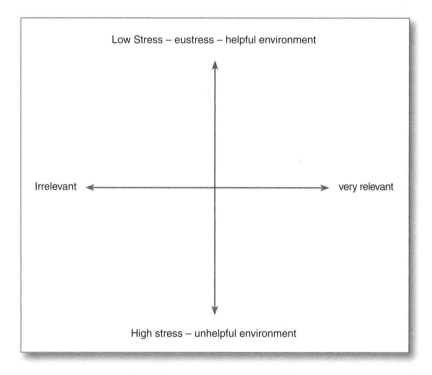

As we read in the chapter regarding emotions, if we feel threatened (part of a stressful environment), a biological reaction occurs deep within the brain that inhibits certain kinds of thinking, especially the kind of thinking we want our students to engage in at school, the critical thinking of the prefrontal cortex. In an environment that is highly stressful, energy that could be used to fire up the frontal lobes is shunted to the emotion and survival regions in the brain.

In opposition to this scenario is the case of the environment that has just enough stress to provide motivation (eustress) while including the kind of support that provides the encouragement sometimes needed when processing (Willingham, 2009).

This is one good reason for instructional leaders to get to know their staff and what makes them tick (including what might be perceived as a threat) and for teachers to get to know their students. One staff member may relish speaking in front of a group to explain or teach or tell a story, while another may see that event as extraordinarily stressful. When instructional leaders know their staff, they know who might feel threatened by such an environment and what might be done to ameliorate the feeling of threat, as well as who might see that environment as supportive and engaging. Therefore, comfort with the environment (the degree of perceived stress) is incredibly important when it comes to processing.

Relevance is the other axis of our graph. A high degree of relevance provides learners with a *reason* to process. This, in turn, encourages and motivates learners to make connections, maintain intellectual flexibility, and persist in their processing when things become complex. If these two dimensions, relevance and environment, are used as filters for processing, planning, learning, and instruction can flourish. As an instructional leader, finding concrete ways to answer the question, "How is this going to help kids?" can be an effective tool for finding or enhancing the relevance in content to be shared with teachers.

THE NEUROSCIENCE BEHIND PROCESSING—AN ANALOGY

In a talk he gave for Learning & the Brain Society in San Francisco last year, John Medina, director of the Brain Center for Applied Learning Research at Seattle Pacific University and author of *Brain Rules* (2008), made a statement that gave the entire audience pause. He said, "If we knew everything about the processing that goes on in our brains that enables us to pick up a glass of water and drink it, it would be a miraculous feat" (Medina, 2009). He went on to describe the inherent complexities that exist in the quest to discover exactly how our brains process thought and action. That caveat stated, I believe when we combine some of the scientific evidence with our empirical understanding of processing, we can do much to improve our current practice (see Figure 4.1).

During a processing event, brain cells, called neurons, communicate through an electro-chemical cascade. This is sometimes referred to as "firing," as there is an element of electricity involved. When people process, they access various parts of their brain, some areas farther apart than others, and some areas very close together. During processing, a track, or pathway, of neurons forms. This is what is referred to as "neural networks." If you imagine yourself learning something for the very first time, you are processing and establishing a new neural network, drawing from all different parts of your brain and memory systems. With

Figure 4.1 How Neurons Communicate

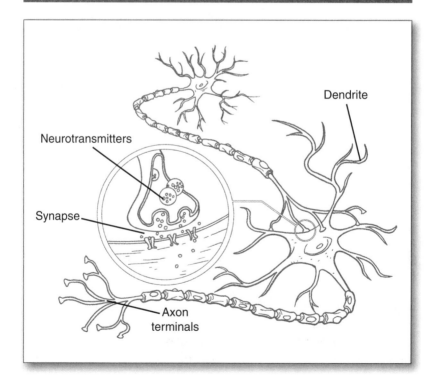

the advent of Diffusion Tensor Imaging, we can now actually take pictures of these pathways in the brain.

In a first-time processing and learning event, these neural networks may be very fragile, like a footpath made the very first time a person walks through a meadow. After that first crossing, all that is left in a person's wake is a faint trace of footsteps that, with a little time, could disappear completely. That's kind of like a first-time processing event with regard to a person's neural networks. Now, if the person crosses back over that same path again (repetition), especially in a short amount of time (distributed practice), the footpath will become a little easier to see and use (the person remembers). With more and more use, the footpath may become a dirt road. Along the way, the person would be starting to notice the interesting parts of the path, where it gets bumpy or where puddles form when it rains. The person might even begin to avoid certain areas because he has discovered a better route, free of puddles. With even more use, that dirt road might eventually become a paved road. Where someone could once only walk, he can now drive a car, getting across that meadow with much greater speed and ease. Eventually, that paved road may become part of a super-highway, with on-ramps and off-ramps that can take people from one area of the state to another with a simple turn of the wheel.

In this analogy, processing is compared to going from creating a faint footpath to establishing a superhighway of thought. This is why experts in different fields can make rich connections to seemingly unconnected ideas. They have such rich and prolific neural networks that they have built superhighways where on-ramps and off-ramps abound. This relates to the earlier example of the instructional leader who can spend limited time in a classroom and walk out with vital information in the form of feedback for the teacher.

Whether we are learning something for the first time as novices or experts adding to our already rich neural networks, there are a few things for the instructional leader to keep in mind in terms of input for effective processing. Because the brain begins to set patterns of thought known as neural networks when we learn, we need to be aware that designing learning experiences that include different modalities during the input phase will potentially enrich these networks. For instance, if teachers want their students to learn about the constitution by using some effective processing tenets, they are going to want to provide multimodal input. This might include showing students a model of the real thing (kinesthetic and visual), showing them an image of the real thing (visual), having students talk about it, or allowing them to hear an excerpt of the constitution read aloud (auditory). This way, students are given the benefit of multiple pathways to access and use in order to make sense of the information during processing and later recall. This concept can be compared to how much easier it is to get to major cities because there are so many highways, railways, and airline flights that begin and terminate in big cities. The more routes that are created in the brain during the input phase, the easier the output phase will be (National Research Council, 1999). (See Figure 4.2.)

BRAIN STRUCTURES, FUNCTIONS, AND PROCESSING

Dr. James Zull, a professor of neurobiology, wrote a book about processing titled *The Art of Changing the Brain* (2002). It is a fascinating look at the biological underpinnings of learning or processing cycles. In his book, he takes the reader through his

Figure 4.2   Neural Network

theories on processing in what he refers to as phases of a cycle the brain goes through during processing. The connection between the biology of processing and the brain regions involved is both compelling and helpful for the instructional leader looking for evidence of effective processing.

Zull's model draws from the work of David Kolb, John Dewey, and Jean Piaget, and it includes four phases: concrete experience, reflection, abstraction, and active testing. During a concrete experience, people gather data through their senses. Their eyes, ears, hands, nose, and mouth are helpful data gatherers. These parts of the body are designed to enable people to understand their surroundings quickly and effectively. During any concrete experience, there is a barrage of data coming at us, and thankfully, our brains are usually able to filter the pertinent data from the unimportant. For instance, if you are in a meeting and suddenly become consciously aware of all the data your sensory system is taking in, you might go mad. Picture becoming consciously aware of the part of your shoe that is pinching your heel, or the scratchy fibers in the scarf around your neck, or the flickering of the fluorescent lights in the office, or the whir, rings, and buzzes occurring in the rooms down the hallway. Now layer upon that your need to process the information given by the person running the meeting. So, your brain mercifully filters out much of the surrounding data you receive.

Sensory organs are the data collectors of this small percentage (1–2%) of data that makes it into a person's conscious awareness. This data is then sent to the thalamus, an internal relay station in the brain, where it is then sent to the appropriate cortical regions where it is gathered, tagged, and sorted. This might be called the input phase of processing, where consideration of our two aforementioned filters is critical.

In Zull's model, the processing continues with reflective observation, when the brain attempts to make meaning out of the data, summarizing, analyzing, and integrating information into the existing mental model, or neural network. People also recall memories of the topic during this phase of processing, making connections to bridge the known to the new. Much of this occurs in areas of the brain that Zull refers to as the back integrative cortex. The back integrative cortex is at the intersection of several lobes (the parietal, occipital, and temporal). The next phase of processing occurs when learners go from receiver of knowledge to creator of their own "versions" of the knowledge. In this phase, a person generates abstract hypotheses, creates new ideas, questions, rephrases, rearranges, and manipulates information in working memory, finding patterns and meaning in the information along the way. Much of this activity occurs in what Zull refers to as the front integrative cortex, residing in the temporal and frontal lobes. One of the hallmarks of the last stage of processing is the active testing of the formed hypothesis, which includes acting upon those ideas. This is when the learner takes action with intention, possibly finds flaws or highlights in the content, and constructs language, either verbally or written, in order to communicate and plan for use in the future. Much of this final phase takes place in the frontal lobes and motor strip. So, how might an instructional leader deliberately plan for this kind of thorough, thoughtful processing among teachers?

PLANNING FOR PROCESSING

If the instructional leader were to take this cycle of processing and apply it to an event, it might look something like this:

Context: You are a principal of a school and would like your staff to have a basic understanding of how negative emotions affect learning and what they can do to ameliorate negative emotions in the classroom. You will be presenting during a portion of a staff development day. The outcome for this presentation is to introduce your staff to how emotions impact learning and begin conversations related to the topic.

The first part of the processing cycle has to do with the two filters mentioned at the beginning of this chapter. To begin planning, the instructional leader must ask these questions: *Is this relevant content?* Absolutely. *In what way(s) does this relevance manifest itself for teachers?* Teachers are in the business of helping students learn. Negative emotions hinder learning; therefore, understanding what and how certain kinds of emotions may hinder learning as well as what can be done to ameliorate the pernicious effect of them will assist teachers' effectiveness. Understanding this might help a teacher see the relevance and open mindsets, which might make the difference between compliance and commitment. *Do we have a learning environment that is psychologically safe during our professional development days?* Yes, the teachers know they are in a supportive environment. This fact is manifested by their collaboration, reflective practices, and ever-present supportive behaviors. Now that the filters have been examined, it's time to take a look at the content with effective processing at the core.

Phase 1—Concrete Learning Experience

In this model, the first phase of processing has to do with a concrete learning experience. Learners are collecting data with their senses, and they must use that to their advantage. Visuals are one of the most effective input sources, so one consideration would be to include some kind of images at the beginning of processing. Since the idea of emotions is a key component of the content for the day, perhaps photographs of faces that elicit different kinds of emotions could serve as a starting point. These images can include video, which would enlist auditory and/or emotional pathways as well. Other possibilities to include might be stories about past experiences or examples of times when people were hampered by negative emotions and why. The instructional leader would prepare this portion of critical input experience using "chunks" of information, broken up into thoughtfully designed components, remembering that learners will be using all their senses to gather this data.

Phase 2—Reflection

The next phase of processing is reflection. To be reflective, learners recall memories of similar experiences from their own schema and consider how they relate to the new learning. At this point, it might be helpful for the leader to lead and guide the processing by asking open-ended questions related to the topic. The leader might ask staff members to reflect upon a time when they may have felt extremely anxious or fearful and how those emotions impacted their ability to process and learn. Now the leader has guided staff members in their processing to help them recall, analyze, and make meaning of this powerful topic.

Phase 3—Abstraction

After reflecting, the learner now transforms from the receiver of knowledge to the creator of his own knowledge, so it will be necessary for teachers to begin to rephrase, question, and find patterns with regard to the topic. Overt linkages are made from the new information to the known. At this point, another guiding question might be framed for the group, such as, "So now that we understand what happens in our bodies when negative emotions erupt, what kinds of hypotheses might you make about what's going on in the brain during negative events?" This will naturally lead the group to the next phase of the processing model, which is the active testing of those newly minted ideas and connections.

Phase 4—Active Testing

The final hallmark of effective processing is the active testing phase, when learners construct language in order to actively test their new ideas and insights. It is during this portion of processing that we want our learners to find potential flaws in their thinking or the content, or points of brilliance to consider, or how this information might be used in the future, to create better lessons, and so forth. During this phase of processing, participants will surely need to write, draw, or verbalize ideas in some way. Language is the currency of cognition. If we don't give teachers or students time and/or guidance in speaking or writing about new ideas or insights, their learning could be truncated.

RESULTS OF EFFECTIVE PROCESSING

When processing is effective with groups, a few things may result. People may become accustomed to being given time to process. This is why making data available before the processing event or sanctioning moments during meetings in which there is quiet, uninterrupted time for processing is key. This might be a new protocol, and therefore, uncomfortable for some people, while others will be incredibly grateful for the opportunity. For those who are uncomfortable with intentional processing, the importance of it may be clarified by informing teachers of the expectations and relevance of the task.

Another thing to notice is that more questions usually emerge from the group. When people can develop questions about a topic, it is an indication that they are beginning to better understand the topic. Be prepared for an influx of questions, some that may be answerable and some that may be unanswerable at the time.

Collaboration can be enhanced when processing events are thoughtfully planned. When teachers are given time and opportunity to verbalize, question, write, ponder, create, dialogue, and discuss during processing events, a deeper understanding and better communication within a team can result. Assumptions may be dispelled, teachers that don't normally participate might begin to, or clarification may be the outcome of effective processing. Results like these can strengthen a team's ability to collaborate effectively (Garmston & Wellman, 2009).

Lastly, another hallmark of effective processing is action. People who are given the skills, opportunity, and resources to process effectively are more likely to end up with action plans as a result. It is through action that we test the hypothesis developed, and it is through action that educators ultimately become more and more efficacious in their craft (BTSA, 2010).

WHAT TO LOOK FOR IN CLASSROOMS: STUDENT PROCESSING

What does processing look like in a classroom? What does it sound like? In this next section, we'll take a look at a few different things the instructional leader might look for in classrooms that support effective processing.

The Use of Multiple Modalities

The more roads into a city, the easier it is going to be to get there. Similarly, the more ways students experience input, the more ways they can make connections to draw from during recall. This is why providing input in multiple ways can be extremely helpful for student processing (Tokuhama-Espinosa, 2011). Instructional leaders want to look for instruction that includes the following: (a) auditory input, such as discussions, music, video clips, and think, pair, share activities; (b) visual input, which includes things like viewing images, reading text, or drawing and labeling; and (c) kinesthetic input, like using realia or movement. Using multiple intelligences may help a teacher embed different modalities in the input, processing, and assessments.

The Use of Specific Structures That Enhance Processing

This section examines some effective methods and materials the instructional leader might bring to a school and later look for in classrooms being observed.

Thinking Maps

Thinking Maps are a set of visual tools that help learners sort and organize their thinking. They represent eight common, high-leverage thinking processes with which students in a K–12 system need proficiency for academic success. They are especially effective when entire schools (or districts) use them to aid student thinking. As a processing tool, Thinking Maps are highly effective. Two critical things occur with their effective implementation in a classroom. One is that students are directly and strategically taught how to think in diverse and strategic ways. Many students don't realize that different kinds of thinking are required for different kinds of problems. Thinking Maps consider that and provide a common language to use when processing, dialoguing, and writing about content.

Classroom Structures That Aid Processing

Another tool that provides a structure for processing in a classroom is Spencer Kagan's conversation chips. These simple little chips, something akin to poker chips, are a clever manipulative that helps to remind teachers as well as students of the importance and fun that processing can afford in a classroom. There are a variety of topics to choose from when purchasing these affordable items, from comprehension questions to processing questions that might help a student with an interview. These can be used quickly and easily in a classroom and provide just enough novelty to increase attention and engagement. Educational leaders like Kate Kinsella and Suzanna Dutrow provide ways for students, in particular English language learners, to embed verbal processing effectively. Structures such as sentence frames and stems can help learners of all kinds become increasingly comfortable using academic language in their processing, ultimately providing a greater degree of specificity in the language and thinking.

Using Drawing for Processing

If a person can draw an idea, he probably understands it. In fact, a quick, effective way to assess a student's knowledge of vocabulary is to ask him to draw the definition of the word. When students know the definition, they will usually be able to draw it.

In the book *The Back of the Napkin* (2008), author Dan Roam explains how drawing can help to spark organized thinking, understanding, and problem solving. Whether students are asked to draw a rendition of their learning after taking notes in a secondary classroom or given a caption from which to draw in an elementary setting, drawing can be a highly effective and natural course to enable many students enhanced processing (and later recall). The instructional leader might want to pull up a chair and pay close attention in a classroom in the event the teacher asks students for a cartoon that explains how the respiratory system works. It just may be the most fascinating part of the leader's day.

Kinesthetic Structures for Processing

When observing instruction that involves a procedure to be learned, the instructional leader should expect to see students' active involvement in the procedure. If the teacher is teaching students how to write capital letters, student processing should include writing capital letters. If the teacher expects students to be able to inspect an essay for powerful lead sentences, student processing should include inspecting an actual essay for powerful lead sentences. The importance of some practice of processes is so great that districts throughout the United States mandate these through policies that include regularly scheduled drills related to emergency events such as fire, tornados, or earthquakes.

Computer-Assisted Processing

Companies such as Scientific Learning and Brainware Safari have developed software that helps students increase their processing power. Through a series of video-game-like programs, this kind of individualized, research-based software has shown great promise for increasing students' speed and accuracy with regard to various cognitive skills.

Time for Processing

Instructional leaders will want to see evidence of time allotted for specific processing in classrooms. There are a few different times during a lesson where processing might be most supportive—basically, somewhere in the middle of the lesson, right after initial input and right before students are expected to show what they know. This does not mean there are only two moments that students are given opportunities to process; it simply serves as a rough rule of thumb to use when considering what is happening during classroom observations. Depending upon what is expected of students during the processing, time needed may fall between a minute or two to several minutes. Instructional leaders should keep this in mind as they watch and observe in classrooms, especially when the teacher's input includes brand new material for students.

Proof of Processing

A quick, easy method that enables an instructional leader to see proof of processing is an exit card. An exit card is a short question or prompt that requires students to process the content of the lesson in some way and generate an answer that promotes their unique perspective and thinking. Exit cards are usually given at the end of a lesson and provide the student with extra processing and the teacher with proof of student processing and understanding.

PROMISING PRACTICES WITH PROFESSIONAL DEVELOPMENT

When instructional leaders present information, they should give adults time and, if necessary, guidance, in processing. They will know a group needs more guidance with processing if no active testing is occurring after processing events. Processing is more than just giving people a little time before a break to collect their thoughts or two minutes at the end of the day to reflect on what they liked the most. Careful processing can lead to a gold mine of new ideas, creativity, and action plans. Processing can make the difference between effective implementation of methods and merely good intentions.

When delivering information that requires careful processing, think back to Zull's four stages. The first stage is where we gather data from different sensory systems. Questions that might be used during or after this stage include these: *What do you notice? What do you see or hear? So what?* The second stage is where we begin to recall memories of concepts that remind us of the new learning. Questions that might be used during this phase include these: *Does this remind you of anything? If so, what?* The third phase is where we become creators of new knowledge, beginning to question, analyze, and find potential flaws or brilliance in the idea. Questions that might be used during this stage include these: *Do any patterns emerge? How does this compare to your past understanding of it? What might be a flaw or stumbling block? What about this might remove barriers? What questions emerge when you think about this?* The fourth stage is acting upon our newfound knowledge. Questions that might be used during this stage include these: *How might you test your hypothesis with regard to this? How would we know if this was the case? How might we find out . . . ? What are your thoughts on how to best implement . . . ?*

No professional development is complete without time to process. Processing helps us deepen understanding and ultimately improve our craft.

WHAT TO LOOK FOR IN A LESSON PLAN

When examining a lesson plan, processing events should be intentional, strategic, and related to the learning target or outcome. No matter what kind of lesson plan format or template a teacher uses, look for specific actions that are called upon for students to process. The list of possible processing activities in the tables found at the end of this chapter (see Tables 4.1–4.5) might provide a good starting place for teachers to incorporate intentional processing events.

Processing will occur at different points throughout a lesson, and depending on the topic and content, it may take center stage. If the lesson is an introduction to a topic, at the beginning of a unit of study, perhaps much of the processing will revolve around tapping into schema and prior knowledge or relating the new information to known information, in order to build a strong foundation of understanding basic ideas.

If the lesson's learning target is one of comparing and contrasting, it may require processing that includes several different phases. In a lesson like this, it might be a good idea for students to have access to a graphic organizer to help them organize the differentiated thinking that will be required to complete such a complex task.

If the lesson's learning target is one of self-assessing students' new knowledge, the teacher might consider having some guided questions on the board to serve as a scaffold for this kind of vital processing. In any case, an effective lesson plan will contain elements that assist students in the completion of effective processing.

LESSON PLANS, UNIT PLANS, AND CURRICULUMS THAT ATTEND TO PROCESSING

One of the roles of an instructional leader is that of an instructional resource. This means that teachers can count on instructional leaders to be able to examine lessons, units, and curriculums and communicate their thoughts on potential flaws or points of effectiveness in such documents. With regard to processing, there are a few things an instructional leader should keep in mind: (a) the way the learning experience is designed to promote relevance to the learners, (b) multimodal ways in which input is delivered, (c) the way deliberate points are incorporated during lessons, units, or curriculums where effective processing activities occur for students, and (d) ways in which processing and learning is made evident, often found in formative assessments that measure the formation understanding.

CONNECTING INSTRUCTIONAL LEADER KNOWLEDGE AND SKILL SETS TO UNDERSTANDING PROCESSING

Resource Provider

The instructional leader that can be counted on to evaluate lessons, units, and other kinds of curriculums for their alignment with brain-compatible processing strategies is a valuable member of any learning organization. Understanding how the human brain processes information allows the instructional leader a lens through which to examine not only curriculums but other practices at a school site as well.

Instructional Resource

When instructional leaders know the hallmarks of effective processing, they will be able to recognize and record critical information and feedback for the classroom teachers they observe. They will also be able to incorporate deliberate processing strategies, like scaffolded questions and structures that deepen thinking in their personal and professional learning and presentations to staff or colleagues that will manifest in deeper understanding, increased critical thinking, and strategic action plans. In Table 4.1, the instructional leader will find a rubric to use with teachers that might help improve processing in classrooms and staffrooms.

Good Communicator

Processing is an integral part of effective communication. When instructional leaders understand what is needed from their staff, colleagues, and students to best process material, they can proactively plan ahead to incorporate elements in written and verbal communication. Some effective methods include explicitly linking the relevance of what is to be learned to the audience's world and assuring an environment of motivating eustress. Stopping points may be found in presentations of new material, where deliberate processing questions or activities can be embedded to encourage deeper thinking or action plans with regard to the learning. Finally, instructional leaders that understand processing know that whether using verbal or written communication, processing takes time, more for some, less for others. Incorporating time for processing will encourage the kinds of critical, creative thinking and action plans that are desperately needed from educators today.

In the following segment of text, a classroom vignette shows how one teacher makes the most of effective processing in the classroom. The wording in italics is like having a whisper coach in the classroom, helping make overt links to the research behind effective processing and how it manifests in the classroom. The elapsed time is bolded, italicized, and underlined.

SAMPLE OBSERVATION OF HOW
A TEACHER EMBEDS THE PRINCIPLE

Teacher: Third grade

Time of day and subject: 10:00–10:20 AM, *English Language Arts*

Learning target: English Language Development—Vocabulary

Time observed: 13 minutes

The lesson is just beginning as you walk into the class-room. The class is comprised of English language learners, all in a similar band of proficiency. It is apparent that the routines and procedures in the class are internalized by students in the class. Their responses are quick and they fluidly integrate the methods the teacher uses. The teacher projects images, color-coded words, and phrases all inside a graphic organizer on a Smart Board. *This takes advantage of multiple mode of input (visual and auditory).*

Students are going to read an article about a topic they chose, and there are some important words in the article that are linchpins for their understanding, so they all understand the purpose and relevance in their learning. The students had been given the opportunity to choose the topic, and the classroom climate is one of respect and safety. *The two filters of relevance and environment were taken care of. The teacher deliberately planned to heighten the relevance of this learning for her students by allowing them to choose the topic for their article and finding the vocabulary they needed to comprehend the chosen reading.*

10:00—The lesson begins as the teacher shares a student-friendly definition of a vocabulary word, along with an image of the word with the class. *The teacher is tapping into her students' neural networks here, to find a starting place for connecting to the new word (the word is* sedentary*).* The student-friendly definition is this: "Sedentary is a word used to describe a lazy person, with no energetic vibe." The teacher intentionally incorporates a rhythm to the definition, along with the student-friendly definition. She then projects an image of a cartoon couch potato. *This shows an adherence to the understanding that in this phase of processing, students are* *gathering data from as many senses as possible. In this case, visual and (rhythmic) auditory senses were attending.*

She asks them to think about the definition and come up with experiences they recall that match the definition of this new word. *This falls in line with the second phase of the processing model mentioned, where we are beginning to integrate information into our schema or prior neural networks.* She has students volunteer instances that further define the word sedentary, and they come up with a short list of other words that are similar to sedentary, that may fall into their casual registers of language. *This engages students in a social learning experience, where they are talking with peers and negotiating understanding.* **Elapsed time 3 minutes**

10:03—Next, the teacher guides her students to further integrate this new vocabulary word by having them compare the word to other synonyms and antonyms, thereby requiring students to use the thinking process of comparing and contrasting. She then "tests" their ability to distinguish the subtle nuances of the word, which helps clarify misconceptions. She does this by making a statement that students assess as an example of sedentary or not; for example, she might say, "I played tennis" aloud. If it qualifies as an example of sedentary, students say the word aloud when she finishes the statement. If it is not an example of sedentary, students say nothing. *This serves several purposes. One, it puts students into an active processing mode. They have a reason to be listening for understanding because there is an expectation that they will actively engage at the end of the statement. It also serves as a way for the teacher to monitor progress of students during the lesson. It is also encouraging the physical act of speaking or articulating the new word. Lastly, it is novel and engaging for students. It almost seems like a game.* When the teacher makes the statement, "I drove to school," and some students say nothing, while a few others say sedentary, she uses that opportunity to ask a probing question of the group. "That's interesting, Juan. Could you help us understand why you didn't say anything when I said, 'I drove to school'?" Juan answers that in his family, his dad drives a car with a stick shift, and it seems to him like there's a decent

(Continued)

(Continued)

amount of moving while his dad drives. He says his arm moves the shifter, while his leg seems to be in motion going from the gas to the brake to the clutch quite often. *This was a perfect example of the second phase of integrating material, where nuances and details are parsed out, along with ideas for how this word might relate to concepts. The students' understanding of this new word is deepened in this phase of the lesson. Elapsed time 5 minutes*

10:05—The class then assists the teacher in creating a continuum of synonyms for sedentary on sticky notes in small groups and arranging them in order from subtle to strong. The continuum looked something like this:

Calm lazy inactive sedentary immobile unmoving

This is a good example of students in the third phase of the processing model, where they are beginning to place this information into their own framework of understanding, discovering the subtleties and nuances of the word and beginning to make connections about possible uses of the word either in writing or in their own speaking. Elapsed time 8 minutes

10:08—Finally, the teacher has students brainstorm ways to complete the following sentence stems:

"I think one way to diminish a sedentary lifestyle is to _____."

"Sedentary! How in the world could you consider _____ to be sedentary?"

This final phase of processing allows for students to practice speaking the new vocabulary word, and it allows them to actively test their new hypothesis regarding the meaning of the word, all the while using a naturally engaging and meaningful protocol— learning with others in a social setting. Elapsed time 11 minutes

The teacher closes the lesson by having students complete an exit card where they write down where, why, and when they might use the word sedentary in the future. *Again, this is evidence of processing in which students are having to use their new knowledge to test a hypothesis of sorts, which falls in line with the last stage of processing that Zull's work describes. Elapsed time 13 minutes*

WHAT ARE SOME OF THE THINGS THE TEACHER DID TO TAKE ADVANTAGE OF HOW WE PROCESS?

- The teacher planned deliberate processing structures during points of the lesson.

- The teacher used the filters of relevance and environment effectively.

- The teacher provided input in multiple modalities (auditory, visual, kinesthetic. and rhythmic).

- The teacher guided students to recall other experiences or knowledge about the subject—tapping prior knowledge from the outset.

- The teacher encouraged students to form hypotheses about their understanding of the new vocabulary word and test it through conversation, sticky note activity, and completion of sentence stem.

- The teacher enabled students to show proof of processing through several different activities during the lesson.

- The lesson required students to think about how they might use this word in the future—engaging students in active testing of new knowledge.

CHAPTER SUMMARY

Processing can be enhanced or hampered by two filters: relevance and environment. When there is ample relevance and the environment is positive, processing can be more effective. The opposite is true if these two filters are flawed in some way.

Processing involves neurons. Neurons communicate through an electro-chemical cascade and grow to form neural networks or pathways that serve as our mental models and memories. The richer the neural networks in a person's brain surrounding a topic, the more expert that person probably is on the topic; and conversely, the sparser the neural networks, the less expert a person probably is on the topic. Zull developed a theory about how we process. His four-phase model includes concrete experience, reflection, abstraction, and active testing. Each phase elicits different brain structures and functions.

There are ways to effectively plan for processing events, as well as ways classroom teachers can embed effective processing structures in their instruction. A few of these ways include using multiple modalities during input, with structures like Thinking Maps, to help organize thinking, and using drawing to problem solve.

Using the information from this chapter, instructional leaders can provide professional development to increase their staff's understanding and implementation of effective processing. Structures and methods that support processing in lesson plans, unit plans, and potential textbooks might include specific and deliberate times at which students are asked to process in ways that make the material relevant, meaningful, and comprehensible.

POSTASSESSMENT CHAPTER 4—THE POWER OF PROCESSING

1. I can communicate the relationship between neural networks and processing.
2. I can share information with my staff about what factors enhance processing.
3. I can apply my understanding of processing to my work as an instructional leader.
4. I can analyze a lesson plan for adequate processing protocols.
5. I can apply the information about processing to what I observe during instruction.

QUESTIONS FOR STUDY GROUP

1. Sometimes teachers are reticent to implement different kinds of processing events in the classroom because of the time it takes. How might you as a leader effectively communicate the reason why "go slow to go fast" works with regard to processing in the classroom?
2. In your current position, what kinds of evidence do you see of effective processing?
3. Where do you see this occurring?
4. How might you teach, encourage, and develop a culture that embraces effective processing?

Table 4.1 Rubric for Principals—Measuring Effective Processing Methods

Criteria	Beginning	Developing	Practicing	Exemplifying
Understanding the content of attention and engagement **Knowledge, comprehension**	Teacher does not yet know or understand what is meant by processing.	Teacher is just starting his learning about processing and can define it but does not yet connect the information to classroom practice.	Teacher has an understanding of processing and uses a strategy or two from the options given for processing in the classroom.	Teacher has a thorough understanding of processing and embeds time and structures to consistently aid processing in planning and instruction.
Relating ideas from the topic to the classroom and applying them **Analysis, application**	Teacher cannot yet relate ideas or actions from her practice to ideas regarding processing.	Teacher can relate one idea she has learned about processing to her practice and apply it in the classroom.	Teacher takes ideas about processing and uses them, at times resulting in effective lesson design and instruction.	Teacher takes many ideas about processing and consistently applies them in lessons. A correlation exists between this application and increased student engagement, recall, and achievement.
Determining which methods and strategies will best enhance attention and engagement in different situations **Application, synthesis, evaluation**	Teacher does not yet apply the methods that help students effectively process material.	Teacher experiments with processing strategies or in a limited manner, with support.	Teacher regularly embeds processing strategies in his planning and instruction.	Teacher consistently and deliberately embeds effective processing strategies in her instruction and planning and measures effectiveness in some way.

Table 4.2 Effective Processing Structures

Processing issue	Ineffective Strategies	Instead . . .
Processing *time*	Students are given inadequate time to process material.	For each concept, plan for a specific amount of time and structures to process the information.
Processing *timing*	Students are asked to process new information for homework.	Students process new information in class before leaving. This helps guide the process and checks for understanding to prevent misconceptions.
Processing *structure*	Students use a verbal processing structure to process a procedure.	Write down the ideal statement or action a student would make or perform to show mastery, then design your processing structure to equip them for exactly that.
Processing *structure*	Students are asked to copy what the teacher wrote on the board.	Have students consider the *model* provided by the teacher and examine for sense making and how it fits into their current mental model. Then have students generate *their own* example or model.
Processing *structure*	Teacher assumes students process effectively during a think, pair, share activity without checking for accuracy.	Give students specific targets to process when incorporating a think, pair, share activity. Instead of using the phrase, "talk to your partners about this," use a specific, deliberate phrase like, "give your partner two reasons why you think the character was courageous."
Processing *structure*	Teacher jumps into a new unit without examining current mental models and schema in the classroom.	Have students complete a circle map (one of the Thinking Maps) that enables them to brainstorm and list words, phrases, and images of how they currently define the concept to be learned. Have students share their circle maps publicly as well.
Processing *timing*	Teacher takes up too much time for processing; ends up wasting precious time.	Keep your finger on the pulse of how long certain processing strategies and concepts are required with students and challenge them to be succinct at times. Talking takes less time; writing takes more time. When writing, sometimes forcing limited words can increase processing effectiveness.
Processing *structures*	Teachers say, "Any questions?"	Instead say, "What are some questions you have?" or "Let me hear some questions from you." This assumes students have questions and will elicit deeper processing.

Table 4.3   Promising Processing Practices

- Using multimodal approaches
  - Process through talking
- Using think/pair/share activities
- Using learning appointments
- Using one-minute lectures
  - Process through writing
- Using think/pair/write/share activities
- Using six-word summaries
- Using jumbled sentences—having three students write one word each on sticky notes, then having students create a sentence using each word given
- Sticky note reflections—because of the limited writing space, this forces students to summarize their thinking effectively
  - Process through drawing
- Using icons in a flow chart
- Using a graphic organizer—create a Thinking Map
- Using cartoons with captions
  - Process through movement
- Putting a movement to an idea
- Completing a word sort with an explanation or debrief
- Using picture movements that relate to the concept
- Creating an analogy
- Creating a metaphor
- Coming up with questions related to topic
- Creating a multiple-choice test item for the topic
- Creating a "Top Ten" list for the topic
- "Picking a fight"—playing devil's advocate about the idea/concept
- Writing a list
- Creating a "how to" flow chart
- Developing a hypothesis with a rationale
- Asking, "What do you see, hear, feel, think?"
- Asking, "How is your understanding now different than this morning?"
- Using sentence frames for language
- Using a T-chart—"What we know" and "How we know it"
- Using guided questions for phases of processing
- Using vocabulary in context

Table 4.4   Aligning Processing Strategies to the Learning Cycle

Questions for Processing

In Phase 1: (collecting data from senses)
- What is it that you notice?
- Describe what you see/hear/feel, etc.
- What are you observing?

In Phase 2: (integrating information)
- Does this remind you of something you are already familiar with? If so, what?
- How does this fit with what you already know?
- What does this remind you of?

In Phase 3: (integrating and analyzing information)
- How is this different from what you already know?
- What patterns do you see emerging from this?
- Why do you believe this to be so?

In Phase 4: (testing hypothesis)
- How might you prove this?
- What might be the reason for this?
- What might happen if . . . ?

Table 4.5   Additional Resources to Find Out More About Processing

Books:

The Art of Changing the Brain—James Zull (2002)

How People Learn—National Research Council (1999)

Quantum Teaching—DePorter, Reardon, & Singer-Nourie (1999)

How the Brain Learns—Sousa (2006)

12 Brain/Mind Learning Principles in Action—Caine, Caine, McClintic, & Klimek (2009)

The Art and Science of Teaching—Marzano (2007)

Cognitive Coaching: A Foundation for Renaissance Schools—Costa and Garmston (2002)

A Field Guide to Using Visual Tools—Hyerle (2000)

Visual Tools for Transforming Information Into Knowledge—Hyerle (2009)

Computer Software and Training That Assist Student Processing:

Brainware Safari—software that improves processing speed

FastForward—software by Scientific Learning that improves processing speed

Thinking Maps—"8 Visual Tools to Organize Thinking and Facilitate Processing"—Training Through Thinking Maps, Inc.

CHAPTER 5

Feedback

In giving advice seek to help, not please.

—Solon, 559 BC

HOW UNDERSTANDING FEEDBACK HELPS THE INSTRUCTIONAL LEADER

Delivering feedback to teachers in effective ways can positively impact instruction, communication, and school climate. To do this, an instructional leader needs to know what to look for in classrooms, how to archive this information, and finally, how to successfully provide feedback to teachers. This chapter will help the instructional leader achieve these skills as well as understand why feedback makes such a big difference for a learner.

Have you ever . . .

- *Spent a lot of effort and time on a project only to find out you were on the wrong track?*
- *Been motivated after receiving a positive remark regarding its potential or impact?*

UNTIMELY FEEDBACK

Years ago, in an art class, we were given an assignment of creating a self-portrait without using an image of one's face. We were given several days to complete our work. I created a self-portrait through song lyrics. As our work became more complete, the teacher occasionally viewed it. When he didn't give me feedback, I figured I was on the right track.

During the critique, the teacher looked at my work and grimaced. He then told me how off track I was and clarified what he wanted. I was frustrated and demotivated. I had invested time, effort, and creative energy on this work, and I had grown fond of it. In fact, I was already gathering evidence in my brain about why my wrong track made more sense than his version.

These situations can result in an unreasonable cleaving to one's work. When we invest time and effort in something, its perceived value increases for us (Brafman, 2008). To later find out the absence of its value to others can create a psychological conflict. This can be avoided through the use of feedback.

FEEDBACK THAT ENCOURAGES
AND MOTIVATES

Feedback can provide motivation and spur creativity and collaboration. This occurred when teachers from the Silver Valley school district in Silver Valley, California, completed the arduous task of revising the district's report card and realized this new standards-based system warranted an informational handbook for parents and community.

After being given time to brainstorm content needed for the handbook, the teachers began their work of writing, researching, verifying information, and clarifying educational concepts for parents and community. Feedback came frequently and in various forms, because a high degree of importance was placed on expressing a common voice. Frequently, members of this team asked the group for feedback in order to make sure they were all on the right track.

I watched as motivation increased. Each time feedback was given, their task, purpose, and vision was further clarified. Feedback occurred through conversation, writing, and at points, demonstration. Although at first frequent feedback was necessary, as they clarified and continued their work, the need abated. Because of the feedback, they felt comfortable giving and receiving, and their work was enhanced and their product was superior.

WHAT IS FEEDBACK?

Feedback is data that serves to inform future steps. We give and receive various kinds of feedback all day long. When our spouse comes home with a scowl and furrowed brow, that's feedback. When a teacher pops his head in your office to say, "Have a good weekend," that's feedback. When a student is absent 35% of the time, that's feedback. Feedback is incredibly important when it comes to deciding what to do next.

WHAT'S GOING ON IN OUR BRAINS DURING FEEDBACK?

Feedback can be like Miracle-Gro for the learning cycle. During a learning cycle, people are making decisions and choosing what data is important and what is inconsequential. Think of riding a bike. Some elements of this process provide more critical feedback than others. For instance, when riding a bike, the ground that is traveled on provides feedback to the rider's body, sending the brain data that tells the rider to turn, slow down, or lean one way or the other. Without the feedback from the ground, riding a bike would be incredibly frustrating. This is why some children who experience sensory integration disorders can find these kinds of activities frustrating or even terrifying. They are missing a key piece of feedback that other people receive without even trying. In a learning event, feedback might take the form of being able to see a clear model, not in order to copy it, but in order to make sure the person is on the right track.

Learning is an active process—dendrites and axons are physically growing and connecting in this process. When given feedback (especially of a correct response), a student gets a boost of a learning-friendly neurotransmitter, dopamine. This then promotes motivation, memory, focus, and pleasure (Willis, 2010). It's no wonder human beings have an innate appreciation for feedback. It helps us survive and thrive.

TIGHT AND LOOSE FEEDBACK

Feedback exists on a continuum, from tightly aligned to a task and very frequent, to loosely aligned and infrequent. An analogy that works to further understand feedback is to think of one side of the continuum, like using a GPS system in your car on the streets of an unknown city (this is the tightly aligned and extremely frequent side), and the other side being the use of a compass.

If a driver is using a GPS, there is usually a lot of feedback given very frequently. Some GPS devices announce when and where to turn in as little as 300-foot increments. Drivers know, within a few seconds, if they have turned the wrong way, and the GPS gives corrective directions to get drivers back on their correct route. For someone who is geographically challenged, the use of a GPS in an unknown city is a godsend. It is like having a security blanket, always right there with the right answer. There are certain conditions where the use of a GPS might be exceptionally helpful, like when the driver is on a tight schedule or if the driver is traveling through a dangerous part of a city. These are times when tightly aligned, frequent feedback is important and valued. Feedback in these kinds of circumstances can serve to curtail fear.

Then there are times when drivers turn off their GPS devices because their previous gratitude transforms into annoyance. If a driver has gotten to know the streets, shortcuts and creative routes can emerge, and the need for constant feedback stops. In this context, a driver might only refer to the compass in the rearview mirror. It shows when the car is headed north, south, east, or west. It provides a driver with just enough information, nothing more and nothing less. Therefore, there is an important relationship between the amount and frequency of feedback needed and the competence and confidence of the learner.

Now take that analogy, and apply it to the classroom or staffroom. There are times when teachers want and probably need the GPS version of feedback. Like in the analogy, those times are when the stakes feel high, fear is present, emotions are elevated, and time is of the essence.

A time when compass feedback is warranted might be when an instructional leader already has a deep understanding of a teacher's practice, and it's impeccable. The evidence comes through each and every time the teacher is in the classroom. Students are productively engaged, collaborating, sharing, and learning on a consistent basis. This teacher probably doesn't need frequent feedback about his practice with classroom management. A grateful (compass) observation might be left in the form of a short note on his desk, but a detailed collection of why this classroom management is exemplary is unnecessary. There is probably an area in the teacher's repertoire that he is still trying to refine or improve. This might be the area where tighter, more specific feedback would be most helpful.

CORRELATION BETWEEN AMOUNT OF FEEDBACK AND DISTANCE TO LEARNING GOAL

There is a correlation between amount of feedback needed and distance from the learning goal (Stiggins et al., 2004). If a student is two grade levels below in her reading, she will need much more feedback in frequent doses compared to the child who is at or above grade level with his reading. Those that need more growth need more feedback. In classrooms, when might GPS feedback be warranted? The idea time is when emotions run high, time limits loom, or competency is minimal. GPS feedback can help struggling learners out of their educational rut, and with time and effort, it can be reduced in frequency and alignment as the students make necessary gains.

DIFFERENT KINDS OF FEEDBACK

There are different ways to give and receive feedback. These are verbally, in written form, or through a demonstration. There are contexts in which each of these kinds of feedback is most effective. If immediate and lengthy feedback is necessary, verbal feedback is probably the best choice.

WRITTEN FEEDBACK

Use written feedback when a person needs to analyze the feedback, as in the feedback a teacher receives after a formal observation. Although written feedback takes more time to deliver than verbal feedback, it is a good tool to use when asking for a change in practice. Written feedback helps information go from working memory to long-term storage, and it serves as an archive for both the giver and the receiver of the information (Brookhart, 2008).

DEMONSTRATION AS FEEDBACK

Demonstrations can serve as valuable feedback, especially when the content to be learned is procedural. Whether the procedure is filling out the new, online report card, or learning how to indent, a demonstration can provide beneficial feedback because the learner sees the procedure which helps to contextualize and make it applicable. After a demonstration, clarifying questions can be asked to ensure understanding.

ELEMENTS OF EFFECTIVE FEEDBACK

In the book, *How to Give Effective Feedback to Your Students* (2008), Susan Brookhart lists elements to consider when using different feedback strategies, in which contexts they are most effective, and recommendations for use. Feedback timing, amount of feedback, the mode of feedback (mentioned earlier), the audience, the focus of the feedback, the function of the feedback, and the valence of the feedback are all elements that the instructional leader can and should consider before collecting or giving feedback to teachers.

EMOTIONAL VALENCE OF FEEDBACK

When we experience an event that evokes strong negative emotions, often, survival responses kick in, and we might not be able to access critical thinking effectively. The purpose of giving feedback is to improve practice, so when instructional leaders give teachers feedback, they will want to do so in a way that *enhances* critical thinking, not shuts it down. It is important to learn the art of giving feedback in a way that is realistic and direct but doesn't demoralize the receiver of the feedback. One way to do this is to begin and end on a positive note. Another method that helps to this end is to let data do the talking. Data can take the sting or personalization out of hard-to-hear feedback. When feedback might be hard for the receiver to hear, communicate why it is critical to understand it, how to correct it, and what steps will be taken in support of that correction. When teachers feel like their areas of improvement are vital, improvable, and supported, difficult feedback can be less daunting.

FEEDBACK IN THE STAFFROOM

Giving effective feedback is a hallmark of effective instructional leaders. Feedback can be given to teachers about many different kinds of things, but the two areas that are most applicable in an educational setting have to do with instruction and professionalism.

GIVING FEEDBACK ON INSTRUCTION

When providing teachers with feedback on their instruction, one of the best places to look is the students. Instructional leaders who are gathering data about student learning, how they are responding, and what they are producing, may discover a rich point of reference from which to mine. Leaders need to become observers of students as much, if not more, than observers of teachers (Reeves, 2006). The product of teaching is learning, so, in order to give effective feedback of instruction, one must discover whether or not the teaching produced what it was designed to produce.

In order to do this, an observer must decide what kinds of actions and behaviors can be quantified and measured. This way, when giving feedback to a teacher, the instructional leader can get directly to the heart of the matter, with data to help paint the picture. So let's put this into context.

In regard to what a learner needs to do in order to accurately process and remember material, there are a few things that are fairly quantifiable, such as the following: making eye contact with the person relaying information; verbally expressing themselves when asked to participate in a think, pair, share, activity; putting pencil to paper when asked to complete a Quick Write and so forth. These are things we can observe without interrupting a student during a lesson, and they might give us feedback about how engaged a student is, but they don't necessarily tell us if students are accurately processing the information. There are two ways to find out if students are accurately learning in a classroom. One way is to ask them questions, and the other way is to examine student products. Asking specific questions of students during a learning event and examining student work can provide terrific feedback.

Following are some of the questions that can be used in order to get information (that later serves as feedback) from students during a learning event:

- What are you learning about?

- Why are you learning about it?

- How are you going to demonstrate your understanding?

- How might you use this learning in the future?

Collecting answers to questions like these can provide data that illustrate components of instruction that a teacher may need to examine that instruction more closely, correct it, or completely overhaul it. To craft questions that will be most valuable for a staff member, an educational leader might look to a mission statement, a schoolwide goal, or a district innovation. Questions might be geared to elicit responses from students that show on which level of Bloom's Taxonomy they are thinking or whether students are using academic vocabulary in a way that promotes formal language registers.

After using a few specific questions to cull an understanding of student thinking, patterns will begin to emerge in both individual teacher's classrooms as well as schoolwide. Regardless of the school's context, feedback that includes student responses is valuable for both teachers and instructional leaders.

Another method to give feedback to teachers is the use of student products. Examining student work is where the buck stops, and it can be one of the most powerful ways for feedback to speak to a teacher without an instructional leader saying a word. No published program or polished PowerPoint presentation quite gets the attention of a teacher like her own students' products.

Using these kinds of methods to gain feedback about instruction is incredibly valuable. The significance of the feedback we gain from examining student work can be an ingredient that propels a mediocre teacher to become a good teacher and a good teacher to become a great one.

FEEDBACK REGARDING PROFESSIONALISM

There are times when educators behave badly. We've probably all witnessed behavior that is unprofessional, embarrassing, or disappointing: sarcastic, mean-spirited comments said aloud; snide, snarky, statements said under someone's breath; or discussion during a colleague's presentation. People might roll their eyes, using that universal symbol for disgust, or treat others as if they are disliked, distrusted, or dismissed. Although these kinds of behavior are rare, they are out there. And they weaken all of the things we aspire to do and be as educators. These behaviors undermine trust, acceptance, and tolerance. They undermine changing and improving and innovating. They undermine the kinds of thinking we need to do to get our schools, and the students within them, where we need them to be.

There are instructional leaders who confront and address these behaviors and leaders who cringe and avoid them. The brain will continue to do whatever helps it survive. If someone who snarls out a nasty remark at a staff meeting gets applause, that behavior is seen as helping that person survive. If, on the other hand, that nasty remark is met with an intervening response by the leader instead of applause, that's a different story. If there is one thing to remember about this section, it is that people who behave in unprofessional ways and get away with it are never going to stop behaving in unprofessional ways. Meanwhile, the people who are made uncomfortable by the eye rollers or the sarcasm are the ones who may have a hard time surviving. And those are usually teachers an instructional leader wants to stick around.

This doesn't necessarily mean that the instructional leader always has to confront every wayward comment or gesture that comes along, regardless of the intensity, but what it does mean is that each time one of these kinds of behaviors rears its ugly head and no one addresses or confronts it, an instructional leader loses a few things, things like trust and respect. Teachers that are put in positions where they are an audience for such unprofessional behaviors lose important things too, things like a feeling of cohesiveness, confidence, efficacy, or hope.

What does this have to do with feedback? People who behave in unprofessional ways *desperately* need feedback, feedback that informs them of exactly what was said or done, why the instructional leader cannot support such behavior, how it affected their colleagues, what the repercussions of this behavior are, and how to alter the behavior in the future. These are not the most comfortable conversations to endure, but they are some of the most important.

The impact of giving needed feedback to teachers regarding their instruction as well as people who behave unprofessionally can be incredibly powerful. The manner in which it is delivered, coupled with timing, focus, and function, need to be considered for the best results.

METHODS OF FEEDBACK IN CLASSROOMS

The following section shares a few ways for giving and getting feedback in the classroom as well as what the instructional leader might look for as examples of such.

Rubrics Are Brain-Compatible

Rubrics give students a foundation of understanding in a clear, concise, visual way. Because rubrics break down a task into pieces, this enables a student to analyze the parts of what is required. Breaking big tasks into smaller chunks can be extremely helpful for students (especially those who may suffer from ADHD) who have difficulty with organization or long, protracted tasks (Ratey, 2008). Rubrics are also highly visual, which can be another helpful tool for students who might need scaffolding with organizing their thinking. (This is especially helpful for those students who are learning English as a second language. See Hyerle, 2000.)

MODELS FOR FEEDBACK

Clear models help students see the whole and how the parts apply. This is a strategy the brain uses (National Urban Alliance, 2009). Wholes (context) taught before parts (content) help people form a global understanding, which in turn aids in recall. Knowledge of both the big picture as well as the details is necessary to demonstrate thorough understanding.

Using models or samples from the students themselves is brain compatible in that it considers what students find meaningful and relevant—their own work. There is a big difference in the response a teacher gets from students when she projects work from a student on the wall as opposed to an artifact created by a publisher. The human brain is a tremendous pattern-seeking device, and students snap to when they notice a familiar pattern that they can personally relate to (Cohen, 2010). That is one of the reasons why using student work as a basis for inspection and examination can be so effective. It's the genuine article, and the genuine article is authentic, more interesting, and ultimately, more valuable.

In the next section, the instructional leader will find what kinds of things to look for in a classroom that constitutes effective feedback.

Using Rubrics for Feedback With Teachers

Rubrics that contain the continuum from novice to expert give learners a kind of road map to excellence. Learners are able to see where they fall on the continuum and what things represent movement toward mastery.

Rubrics are included in each state's evaluation methods for teachers. These documents contain criteria for differentiated levels of skill or performance in teaching domains. Rubrics can be as beneficial when working with teachers as they are in the classroom with students because of the amount of feedback they provide and the substantive conversations they can bring forth.

This book provides rubrics for the instructional leader to use with teachers for each of the brain-compatible principals examined. These were designed to be used as a tool to measure growth and provide a road map for teachers and instructional leaders to use to identify the next level of work. The next section discusses rubrics that may be incorporated into an instructional leader's practice, using either the rubrics provided in the first table at the end of each chapter in this book or those that can be found in each state's department of education documents for teacher evaluation.

One of the first steps to using a rubric as a tool for measurement in a teacher's practice is allowing for time and processing of the contents of the tool. Using methods from Chapter 4, instructional leaders might sanction time at a staff meeting to engage their staff in dialogue and clarification of the contents of the criteria. It is vital that the people who will use the tool as a basis for evaluation purposes as well as the people who will be evaluated have a common and complete understanding of the contents, purpose, and use of the document.

After everyone has a firm grasp of the rubric, teachers can be asked to make some decisions about which portion (on the continuum) matches their practice and why they believe this to be so. Providing evidence in some form and highlighting (and dating) directly on their copy of the rubric can serve several purposes:

(1) It brings the level of awareness about best practices and expectations to a concrete level for teachers and instructional leaders. It goes far beyond talking about best practices. This activity asks teachers and instructional leaders to analyze the contents of the document and then analyze and evaluate their own practice.

(2) This activity may act as a form of eustress for some, because the experience of putting something in writing, (highlighting, dating, and listing evidence) heightens the level of awareness, engagement, and commitment for a teacher. It also serves as an archive to revisit during subsequent conversations with a teacher.

The rubric can then be revisited, however many times makes sense in the situation. If a teacher has a professional goal of improving competency with gaining and keeping students' attention, an instructional leader might want to have the teacher examine the rubric provided in this book at the onset of the goal formation. The leader may then have the teacher revisit the rubric and see if competency has shifted from one column to the next months later. It may then be revisited again at the end of the year. Because of the kind of feedback the rubric serves, there is less subjectivity in the measurement, and improvement becomes less about what a teacher is told to do than what a teacher brings about.

WHAT TO LOOK FOR IN THE CLASSROOM

An effective classroom is filled with feedback, and effective teachers make feedback part of their normal routine. The work that adorns the walls of a classroom, the use of learning progressions, visual rubrics, white boards, student response systems, checklists, and reflections, can all enhance the amount of feedback students in classrooms are able to get and give. The next section describe these methods in a little more detail.

Student–to–Student Feedback

The four walls of a classroom can be a gold mine of feedback. In some teachers' classrooms, students have a place on the wall that they "own." This spot is a place for students to post work they would like to display or get feedback on. If students request feedback, they simply place an index card next to their work. This indicates to classmates, other teachers, the principal, or visitors that this student would like feedback regarding his work. Using the walls of the classroom to enable students to get and receive feedback is helpful in a few ways. First is the feedback itself. Second, this method allows students to internalize the importance of giving and getting feedback and helps them become effective givers of feedback themselves.

Learning Progressions

Learning progressions sequence and break up a complex task into steps, beginning with a less complex step and building upon it as needed. The sequence ends with the complex task completed. It can be an extremely valuable tool for a variety of grades and developmental stages.

Creating a learning progression begins by choosing a standard, or learning target, and completing a hierarchical task analysis. The task is broken down into the subskills and prerequisite knowledge that students need to master at each step in order to master the entire task (or standard). After breaking down the task, the teacher then draws (or uses a digital format) a visual that looks like steps, and inside each of the steps a simple, kid-friendly explanation of the prerequisites is written in an "I can . . . ." statement.

This serves as a tool for students to recognize and archive where they are on the steps to mastery and keep track and monitor their learning.

To contextualize this, let's say the teacher chose the task of being able plan, write, edit, and revise a paragraph, a common standard in elementary schools throughout the country. The learning progression visual might look something like this (see Figure 5.1):

Figure 5.1   Sample Learning Progression

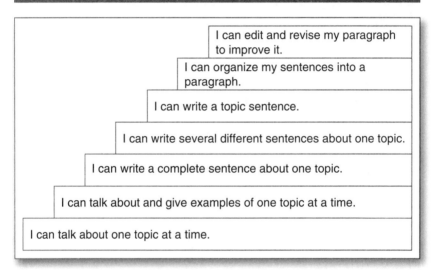

As you can see, each step was built on the subsequent step's mastery, helping students see how writing a paragraph requires cognitive and skill-based steps, with each step an important stepping stone on the path to mastery.

Learning progressions serve as a form of feedback that gives students visual, sequential, and reasonable steps to follow in order to master a task (standard). When students are ready to move to the next level (which is a nice connection with children's knowledge of video games), they bring the teacher *evidence that they have mastered their current level.* This evidence is a valuable form of feedback for the teacher to see that the students are meeting the different demands of the task. Learning progressions are a terrific tool to use at conference time, when students can be given the opportunity to share with parents or guardians where they are in the learning process. Even students who have only been able to color in the first two steps show pride in their improvement and see the connection between effort and progress.

Using this method enhances a student's feedback and motivation. When we feel like we have control of and for our learning, we are more likely to be motivated to master our learning (Stiggins et al., 2004). Our brains are problem-solving machines. Each step in a learning progression can be seen like a little problem to our brains, and because it is broken down into reasonable pieces, we are more likely to maintain our motivation to gain mastery, to get to that top step.

FEEDBACK DURING INSTRUCTION

During instruction, the need, content, and timing of feedback can vary. Often, at the very outset of learning, after some input has been given, feedback needs to be sought from students; this is what we commonly refer to as checking for understanding. Near the beginning of the instruction, it is beneficial for a teacher to know that the students comprehend or can apply what has been taught so far. Deliberately planning to give and get feedback during this phase of instruction does two things: It informs the teacher about which students understand and which students might be faltering in their understanding. This enables the teacher to inject corrective instruction immediately, so that a student doesn't learn something incorrectly. Most teachers know that trying to undo incorrect learning (misconceptions) is much more difficult and time consuming than teaching with a clean slate. This is one of the reasons instructional leaders are always on the lookout for checking for understanding.

A way that a teacher might give and receive feedback during the initial instruction phase, when the potential benefit feedback can bring is very high, is the use of whole class participation methods. This is when and why the use of individual white boards can be so helpful. The use of white boards enables a teacher to see each student's thinking. Teachers can vary what they ask of students using white boards; for example, in math, the teacher may ask students to draw a shape that represents a rhombus. This provides immediate feedback. The teacher instantly knows who understands what a rhombus is and who does not. This also gives students the opportunity to test whether they are on track. This kind of fluid and dynamic assessment during the initial phase of a lesson can provide valuable feedback for both teacher and students.

Individual White Boards and Feedback

The use of white boards relieves anxiety many students feel when being put on the spot to answer a question in front of 30 other students. They are also a novel item, so we attend a little better while using them. When students use a white board, the expectation is clear that they will continue to think, persevere, and attend throughout the lesson. Use of white boards sends several clear messages to students. One is that the teacher wants to know how and what they are thinking and if they understand the content. Another is that participation is nonnegotiable. Lastly, the approach to "learning" as evidenced by three engaged people answering all the questions while 27 others mentally check out is more compliance than reliance.

Student Response Systems

During the next phase of instruction, where students may be trying out their learning, testing hypotheses, or otherwise rehearsing, there are a few other forms of feedback that may be helpful. The use of i-clickers (or some other instant feedback device), five-finger rubrics, and dots are a few notable methods used to benefit student engagement and learning.

I-Clickers

After the initial phase of instruction, what might be called the input phase, students need time to process the material. I-clickers are remote controls that students can use to choose correct answers to questions (think *Who Wants to be a Millionaire*). During this phase of the lesson, a teacher might ask students questions to ensure they are on the right track or to ferret out misconceptions. I-clickers communicate with a laptop and software to create a visual graph of how students respond. The teacher can gain feedback about how the class is doing, as a whole, with their understanding of concepts they are learning. Individual students can also gain immediate feedback as they find out the right answer. I-clickers provide feedback that is anonymous, alleviating the anxiety many feel when unsure about an answer. They are also novel and have elements which might very well turn a history lesson into a game show on the spot.

Five-Finger Rubrics

Five-finger rubrics are helpful in determining students' level of confidence with regard to the subject matter, and although there may be the rare individual whose confidence is unwarranted, most students are spot on with their confidence levels. Students in classrooms where this method is used know what each number stands for. One finger means, "I am unclear about this concept and need help to understand it"; two fingers mean, "I'm a little unclear and might need help to understand it"; three fingers mean, "I'm pretty clear but might have some clarifying questions"; four fingers mean, "I'm clear and ready to charge ahead with my work"; and five fingers mean, "I could teach this concept to someone else." Upon setting students to work after guided practice, this five-finger rubric is a helpful tool to find out which students may need closer supervision and which ones can handle the independence they request.

The Magic of the Dot

I watched Michael Wong, a teacher from the Mt. Baldy school district in Mt. Baldy, California, use the simple method of placing a dot on students' papers, with amazing results. After she had finished the input portion of her lesson, she asked the students to process their new learning by completing a graphic organizer to help them organize their thinking to compare and contrast two concepts. After she gave directions, the students set to work. The industrious nature of the class was impressive after she gave the "start working" signal. It was then that I saw her go to her desk and retrieve a purple marker. I noticed several students watch as she approached them, peering over their shoulders at their work in progress. After a few seconds of analysis, she put a dot on the left side of the paper of one of the students, where the child was filling in the differences between the two stories. As she moved to the next child, she placed a purple dot on that paper as well. As she moved around the room, I watched as students wrote furiously and sat up a little taller in their desks after receiving the feedback of the dot. At one point, she examined a student's paper and failed to place a dot on it. The student immediately responded by asking why he had not received a dot. The teacher was able to let him know that what he had written so far did not constitute similarities. In short, she let the student know he was off track. The student immediately went back to his desk to further inspect his organizer. He came back to the teacher moments later to show her his revised thinking and to see if he was on the right track. He was, and the problem was solved.

At the beginning of the 15-minute time period that the students were given to begin this work, the teacher moved around the room at a brisk pace, placing dots on papers and moving on. As time progressed, she was looking over fewer shoulders and working more with two students than any others. After the students left the classroom to go to lunch, I asked her about the method she was using. She said she started using it out of frustration with interruptions she was having in the classroom one day. It was school picture day and the office was calling the classroom more than usual. Out of frustration, while she was reading over one of her student's papers, the phone rang, so she grabbed a marker out of the student's material box and put a dot on the corner of the child's paper and said, "You are well on your way," and answered the phone.

When the teacher returned from the phone call, a few students were hovering over the girl's paper, asking why she received a dot. Who knew dots could be so captivating for students? In actuality, the power of the dot doesn't come from the fact that it's purple or that it even comes from the teacher. The power of the dot is the fact that it signifies feedback and progress for students. The power of the dot equals the power of feedback.

Checklists Provide Feedback

Feedback at the end of instruction should signal to the student and teacher where students are on their way to mastery, as well as what the next steps are in their progression toward mastery. Kinds of feedback that help during this phase of a lesson include methods such as checklists or cuing questions to use to inspect work, reflections, rubrics, and models (again).

Checklists or cuing questions can be used in cases where students need to include several items in their work. For instance, in math, a checklist might include the following:

- Did you use graph paper?

- Did you show your work?

- Does your answer have an explanation?

In a lesson that requires students to write a constructed response to a science question, the checklist (or cuing questions) might include the following:

- Highlight the words that answer the question directly.

- Highlight the words that give an example of why this is true.

- Highlight the words that indicate how you will use this information in the future.

The completion of a checklist is a way to get students to understand what they have accomplished so far, as well as next steps to complete the assignment. When a teacher requires students to inspect their own work, she is not only helping those students become familiar with owning the responsibility of examining and analyzing their work, she is scaffolding their ability to do so by providing them with the important elements for which to inspect. The use of highlighters can add an effective visual cue for students, so that when students complete their inspection and have only one small streak of bright pink highlighter on their paper, that powerful feedback informs them of their necessary next steps. Methods like these engage and motivate students, which, in turn, help them to expend the effort demanded of critical thinkers.

Reflections for Feedback

Asking students to reflect on a lesson and list the most important things they learned and how they will apply that learning can provide teachers with powerful feedback. If 95% of the reflections mention interest in the same concept, perhaps that signals to the teacher the need to expand that concept or weave that concept into other areas of the curriculum.

At the end of a lesson, a rubric or model can be used as feedback for students. For instance, let's say students had been working on a comic strip to demonstrate their understanding of the historical concept. Although students might still be able to complete the work at home, the teacher could share a sample of a comic strip made by a student in a previous class (that showed a different concept). The teacher could guide the students to see some of the critical features of the comic strip that made it an exemplary product. Students could then compare the model to their own product and refine it where necessary.

Feedback doesn't need to be long, drawn out, or painful (for the giver or receiver). Feedback can be quick, simple, and tremendously effective. Instructional leaders who understand feedback can better serve their teachers through professional development, communication, and the provision of resources.

PROFESSIONAL DEVELOPMENT FOR TEACHING ABOUT FEEDBACK

Once teachers have foundational knowledge about how learning occurs when neurons communicate with one another and that pathways of understanding begin when people are given opportunities to see, talk, write, draw, and think, they are primed to learn more about how feedback can impact their teaching and student learning.

When presenting on feedback, have participants think of a time when they learned something well, and then ask them to complete this stem: "When I learned how to _____, I received _____ feedback." The vast majority of participants will fill in the second blank with words like, frequent, constant, effective, nonjudgmental, detailed, informative, and so forth. Then ask them to choose one side of the room or the other, depending on whether their descriptors were positive or negative. Sometimes, several teachers might say that they learn better with little to no feedback, just like there are people who can smoke three packs a day, never exercise, and live to be 100. But most people end up on the same side of the room. At that point, ask them to turn to someone and converse about when feedback was "just right." The teachers are now primed for learning how to provide effective feedback in the classroom for their students.

Usually, teachers acknowledge that feedback is helpful, but they often see it as complicated, time consuming, and challenging. During professional development about feedback, one of the key responsibilities of the presenter is to ameliorate these feelings by sharing and showing teachers a few simple, effective ways to provide feedback.

WHAT TO LOOK FOR IN
A LESSON PLAN

A lesson plan should denote suggested times and places when the teacher predicts feedback will be most helpful for students, how feedback will be given to students, and the amount that would best serve the population. Just as the initial phases of a lesson might require more frequent feedback, lessons at the beginning of a unit are going to possibly require more frequent, specific feedback than lessons nearer the end of a unit where students are working effectively and independently.

The key here is to consciously determine not only where feedback will most likely be needed by students (and by the teacher) but also the manner in which feedback will be given. Using the sections from this chapter regarding different elements of effective feedback and methods used in classrooms, teachers can gain an understanding of not only when, but how, to provide their students with feedback to equip them for their best next step.

CONNECTING INSTRUCTIONAL
LEADER KNOWLEDGE AND SKILL
SETS TO UNDERSTANDING FEEDBACK

Resource Provider

As an instructional leader, providing concrete resources like student response systems for feedback or budgeting for individual white boards would be a helpful step in increasing feedback in classrooms. Instructional leaders who possess the skills and knowledge regarding feedback methods and the rationale behind them build the capacity of their staff in an incredibly vital area for learning.

Instructional Resource

The instructional leader that recognizes the need and phases of instruction where feedback is most beneficial can assist teachers in planning effective lessons, punctuated by effective feedback. The leader can provide feedback to teachers about their own practice as well as the ways in which students give and receive feedback in the classroom. The leader can assist teachers in locating where they are in their own professional growth using feedback methods, such as the process used to measure proficiency with rubrics, and revisit these rubrics in order to mark teachers' progress in continually improving as educators. The rubric in Table 5.1, found at the end of this chapter, is an effective tool in this way.

Good Communicator

One of the most challenging requirements of an instructional leader is providing valuable feedback in an effective way. When feedback is mostly positive, the job is easy. But when a teacher needs critical feedback, it can be challenging. Instructional leaders who understand the elements of effective feedback, how emotions work (from a previous chapter), how language can be crafted to alleviate anxiety and fear and open minds, and how to choose the best form of feedback (written, verbal, or demonstration) for the specific context are equipped with the vital knowledge and skills necessary to transfer this information to one of their most important practices, giving feedback to teachers that leads to improved practice. Tables 5.2 and 5.3, found at the end of this chapter, provide tips and tools for collecting information and sharing feedback with teachers (see also Figure 5.3).

In the following segment, a classroom vignette shows how one teacher makes the most of giving and getting feedback in the classroom. The wording in italics is like having a whisper coach in the classroom, helping make overt links to the research behind feedback and how it manifests in the classroom. The elapsed time is bolded, italicized, and underlined.

SAMPLE OBSERVATION OF HOW A TEACHER EMBEDS THE PRINCIPLE

Teacher: 10th grade

Subject and time of day: Science—9:45–10:05 AM

Learning target: Student will articulate the difference between independent, dependent, and controlled variables

Time observed: 20 minutes

9:45—You walk into the classroom and the students have been in class for a few minutes. Samples of exemplary student work adorn the walls, along with the rubrics that provide the evidence for their proficiency. There is a large bulletin board where a poster of the learning progressions of how to form a hypothesis is displayed. There are also places on the bulletin board where students have posted work and peers have written feedback on index cards next to it. The teacher is walking around to different students and checking in with them regarding last night's homework while students complete a Likert-type scale survey about the content of the lesson by coming to the board and placing an X under the appropriate number for each survey question. *This shows that the teacher is giving some students feedback on an individual basis regarding homework as well as getting ready to receive feedback from the class as a whole regarding their understanding and confidence about the topic to be learned. The room environment shows embedded visuals that provide feedback for students and teacher.* **__Elapsed time 3 minutes__**

The giant graph that students created with their check marks looked something like Figure 5.2:

Figure 5.2   Sample Student Graph

Circle how confident you are in your understanding of the following:

1 = *Not at all confident*   5 = *Exceedingly confident*

I can name at least three variables related to yesterday's lab:

1	2	3	4	5
	X	XXXX	XX	X
	X	XXX	XX	
	X	XXX	XX	
	X	XXX		
		XXX		

I know the difference between independent, dependent, and controlled variables:

1	2	3	4	5
XXXXX	X	X	X	X
XXXXX	X	X	X	
XXXXX	X			
XXXX				

(Continued)

(Continued)

The teacher has students examine the graph and asks, "What does this data tell us?" *This question serves to help students in their ability to use data as a source of feedback as well as gives students practice in giving feedback.* The teacher calls on a student to articulate her thoughts. She responds, "I think maybe it shows that we are most confident with the first question, the one about naming the three variables from yesterday's lab, probably because it is fresh in our minds." Another student adds, "Yeah, and I think we might need a reminder about the differences between the different kinds of variables, 'cause look at how many Xs are in the 'about what?!' column. Another students adds, "Hey, who are the 'Exceedingly confident' people? Is it the same people on every question?" *This shows a level of engagement and the student's ability to analyze, give, and receive feedback regarding data.* **Elapsed time 5 minutes**

The teacher agrees with some of the comments the students have made and suggests that they do need to sharpen their understanding with some concepts. He then asks his students to stand in a line from the fives on the scale to the ones on the scale, to do a lineup that loosely represents their confidence and knowledge level. He then "folds" the line, which results in the lowest being paired with the highest and the middle highest being paired with the middle lowest. This enables some of the students who might be having the most difficulty to have a partner that has a decent grasp on the subject. He passes individual white boards out to pairs of students and asks them to create a schematic and label some kind of variable. He gives the students a minute to work together and asks them to universally hold up their white boards so he can check to give and get feedback. *This gives the teacher a terrific amount of specific feedback regarding where students are on their way to mastering the standard, while at the same time the students are getting feedback from their teacher about whether they are on track.* **Elapsed time 7 minutes**

The teacher then gives a more difficult task to the students who completed the first task accurately and turns his attention toward a very small group of students and gives them specific, corrective instruction using their drawings on their white boards as examples. After a few minutes, he gives this small group another task and turns his attention to the previous group. This back and forth occurs for about five more minutes. *Aside from providing dynamic differentiated instruction for his group and guiding processing effectively, the teacher is able to use the feedback from students to gauge where they are in their learning progression. At the same time, students are able to get feedback from one another throughout the process.* **Elapsed time 16 minutes**

Now that the teacher has provided specific, differentiated instruction, punctuated by feedback intervals, the students are showing greater confidence and understanding about the learning target. The next portion of the lesson includes a "case study" of a science lab, taken out of a student's science notebook, that he projects onto the white board. The teacher has students inspect this case study for the different kinds of variables. Students are asked to record the variables found in the case study in their own notebooks, providing rationale for each underlined portion, and they underline the variables projected on the white board to check their answers. *This final activity provides the teacher with feedback about where students are in their learning as well as providing students with feedback about whether they are on the right track with their thinking.* **Elapsed time 20 minutes**

WHAT ARE SOME OF THE THINGS THE TEACHER DID TO TAKE ADVANTAGE OF GIVING AND GETTING FEEDBACK?

- Students used the learning progressions poster.

- Students were given "feedback" space in the classroom to post their work.

- Clear models of exemplary work were made available to students.

- The teacher provided individual feedback to some students regarding their homework from the previous night.

- Pairs of students were grouped in a manner that allowed the most challenged students to benefit from their most confident peers.

- The teacher used the Likert-type scale prior to beginning the lesson to gain valuable feedback from the students about specific prior knowledge of the topic.

- The teacher used a whole class participation method (white boards) to gain feedback from students quickly and effectively.

- Students were encouraged to give and receive feedback from one another during the paired activity during the lesson.

- Students completed a case study where they were required to inspect for certain elements related to the learning target and provide rationale for why.

CHAPTER SUMMARY

Feedback is like Miracle-Gro for learners. It provides them with information to keep them on the right track as they progress through the stages of acquiring new knowledge. For these reasons, feedback can serve to assist a learner greatly. It can be loose or tight, depending on the needs of the learner at the time. In instances where a person is unsure or having difficulty with the content, feedback may need to be more frequent and specific. The opposite is true if the learner is confident and advanced in her knowledge and skills.

There are different ways to give and get feedback, including written, verbal, and demonstrations. These different formats work well in various contexts, depending on the needs of the learner and the purpose of the feedback. There are elements of effective feedback that might be considered that include timing, amount, audience, content, function, and emotional valence.

The instructional leader can look for effective real-time feedback in classrooms during observations. Some of these methods might include the following: rubrics, clear models, learning progressions, and whole class participation methods such as white boards, student response systems, checklists, and reflections.

Professional development for feedback includes activities that will help teachers make connections between what they see in their classrooms and already know to be true and what the world of neuroscience tells us is going on in the brain during feedback events. It can also include various methods that a teacher may implement to increase the amount of feedback given and gotten in the classroom.

Instructional leaders who understand this vital principal can serve as a valuable resource to their staff, by finding ways to provide concrete tools that increase the level of feedback for students and teachers. Leaders can provide information to teachers that help them gauge and measure feedback practices in their classroom as well as their professional practice. And finally, instructional leaders who have a firm grasp on this principal can communicate more effectively, because they understand the most important tenets of giving feedback in a way that promotes an open mindset.

POSTASSESSMENT CHAPTER 5–FEEDBACK

1. I can describe what is going on in the brain when a person receives feedback.

2. I can analyze a lesson plan for elements of effective feedback.

3. I can share strategies with others regarding ways to provide feedback.

4. I can recognize and record effective feedback practices during instruction.

5. I can effectively give feedback to teachers.

QUESTIONS FOR STUDY GROUP

1. Reflecting on the current situation at your school site, how often do your students experience effective feedback in the classroom?

2. What are some barriers to giving and receiving effective feedback at your site?

3. How often do your teachers receive effective feedback from their students?

4. How often do teachers receive effective feedback from the instructional leader?

5. If you could design the perfect feedback loop among staff, what would it look like?

6. What might be some next steps to get there?

Table 5.1 Rubric for Principals—Measuring Teacher Knowledge and Skill With Feedback

Criteria	Beginning	Developing	Practicing	Exemplifying
Understanding the topic of feedback **Knowledge, comprehension**	Teacher has not yet acquired the foundational understanding of how feedback works or impacts learning.	Teacher is just starting his learning about how vital feedback is during a learning event.	Teacher has an understanding of how feedback during instruction impacts learning.	Teacher has a thorough understanding of how feedback before, during, and after learning impacts learning and can explain it to others.
Relating and applying ideas from the topic to the classroom **Analysis, application**	Teacher cannot relate ideas or actions from her practice to ideas regarding feedback in the classroom.	Teacher can relate one idea she has learned about giving or receiving feedback in her practice in the classroom.	Teacher takes many ideas about giving or receiving feedback and applies them occasionally in the classroom.	Teacher takes many ideas about giving and receiving feedback and consistently applies them in several contexts in the classroom.
Determining which methods and strategies will best enhance feedback in the classroom **Application, synthesis, evaluation**	Teacher does not yet apply the methods regarding feedback that help enhance student learning.	Teacher experiments with one or two ideas for providing feedback in the classroom.	Teacher regularly embeds some kind of feedback in different aspects of the classroom.	Teacher consistently and deliberately embeds effective methods of giving and receiving feedback in different aspects of the classroom.

Table 5.2 Tips for Giving Different Kinds of Feedback

Kind of Feedback	Tips	
Praise or reinforcing feedback: *Remember to provide specific information about how the action of the teacher had positive results on student learning. Remember, the purpose of giving feedback is to provide data that inform and enhance next steps.*	Instead of: *"I loved that video clip you used at the onset of the lesson."*	Try this: *"Every student in the class appeared to turn their attention to that video clip at the onset of the lesson. Knowing how important both attention and engagement are in the learning cycle, this method, and the content of the video, looked like they served to grab their attention and hold it effectively."*
Suggestions: *Allowing teachers to make professional decisions about next steps builds their capacity and sends a positive presupposition to the teachers regarding their ability to improve.*	Instead of: *"I think it would have been better if you would have allowed the students to repeat the process of finding the subject in each sentence a few more times."*	Try this: *"I noticed that when students were processing the information about what constitutes a subject in the sentence you gave them an opportunity as a class to find the subject in two sentences. Knowing what we know about robust memory making, how might you provide more elaborative rehearsal?"*

(Continued)

Table 5.2 (Continued)

Kind of Feedback	Tips	
Criticism: *When something has occurred during an observation that is unacceptable or detrimental to learning, clear, specific, thoughtful communication is vital. This is the most difficult feedback to relay for most, but it can be done in a way that engenders both clarity and support.*	Instead of: *"You lost your whole class when you made that sarcastic comment to the student in the back row."* (This style of feedback puts the teacher on the defensive.)	Try this: *"When you made the sarcastic comment to the student in the back row (inject actual comment), students responded to you with defensive tones and appeared to disengage from the lesson. Your modeling as a teacher is vital to your students, and knowing the impact sarcasm can have on a student's cognition and emotional valence, I can't support that behavior. What kind of response reflects what we want to see in our students in these instances?"*
Clarifying: *Sometimes an instructional leader might see something going on that is confusing. It's a good idea to begin the feedback for the teacher with clarification of potentially confusing issues.*	Instead of: *"I don't think that having kids look up words in the dictionary is the best way for them to learn vocabulary words. The lack of engagement was palpable."*	Try this: *"I noticed you had students look up words in the dictionary during my observation. Can you help me understand the purpose of this activity?" OR "Can you clarify how this activity fosters engagement or active processing with our students?"* (The teacher might have a reasonable purpose behind using the method, and given the opportunity to clarify, she might put the instructional leader's mind at ease.)

Table 5.3 Feedback Form for the Five Principles

Teacher:	Time and date:
Subject:	Learning target:
Emotionally relevant methods: (positive language used by teacher and students, pleasant aesthetics, positive classroom climate, use of simulations, emotionally relevant content, use of games for learning, use of debates or other method that heightens emotion and/or meaning for students)	**Evidence:**
Processing in the classroom: (deliberate processing structures incorporated before, during, and/or after lesson; questions or cues used to guide or enhance processing; effective chunking of information; multimodal input; relevance embedded into content; enough time to process incorporated into lesson)	**Evidence:**
Memorable instruction: (attention paid to M-space—not too much information for students to hold in working memory at one time, rehearsal and repetition deliberately embedded, meaning and emotion used in instruction and/or planning, attention paid to chunking material)	**Evidence:**
Attention and engagement: (different methods used to capture students' attention when necessary before, during, and/or after the lesson; engaging qualities of work observed: novelty, social learning, humor, authenticity, feedback, clear models, choice, etc.)	**Evidence:**
Feedback in the classroom: (feedback given and/or received in different ways in the classroom, visuals on the walls providing feedback, learning progressions used, whole class participation methods used, such as individual white boards, student responders, etc.)	**Evidence:**
Questions:	
Considerations:	

Figure 5.3   Examining Student Work to Mine Feedback—Flow Chart
Protocol

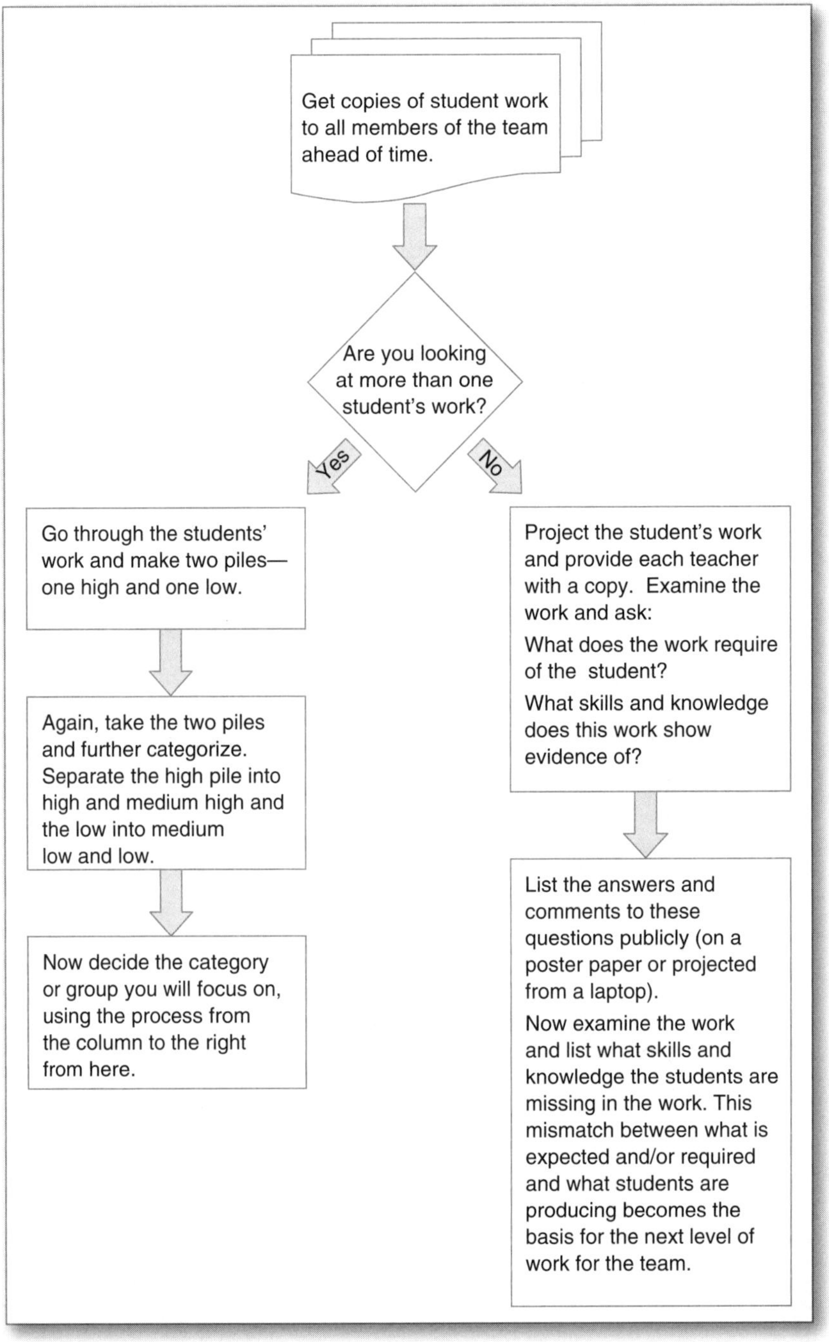

Get copies of student work
to all members of the team
ahead of time.

Are you looking
at more than one
student's work?

Yes

No

Go through the students'
work and make two piles—
one high and one low.

Again, take the two piles
and further categorize.
Separate the high pile into
high and medium high and
the low into medium
low and low.

Now decide the category
or group you will focus on,
using the process from
the column to the right
from here.

Project the student's work
and provide each teacher
with a copy. Examine the
work and ask:

What does the work require
of the student?

What skills and knowledge
does this work show
evidence of?

List the answers and
comments to these
questions publicly (on a
poster paper or projected
from a laptop).

Now examine the work
and list what skills and
knowledge the students are
missing in the work. This
mismatch between what is
expected and/or required
and what students are
producing becomes the
basis for the next level of
work for the team.

CHAPTER 6

Memory

Unless we remember we cannot understand.

—Anonymous

Anyone who has watched a loved one suffer from Alzheimer's disease can describe how distressing it is to witness the loss of memory, and this quote sums up why. Our memory allows us to make connections, learn, and participate in our world. This chapter will help the instructional leader sort out some of the fundamentals of memory formation (encoding) as well as recall (retrieval). Current research about this topic suggests that not only is there a correlation between a good memory and fluid intelligence, but there are ways we can improve memories. Ways in which we can improve memory can be manipulated in a classroom or staffroom to transform the unmemorable to the unforgettable (Cohen, 2010).

HOW UNDERSTANDING
THE WAY MEMORY WORKS
HELPS THE INSTRUCTIONAL LEADER

The point of education is to learn. In order to learn and understand, a person needs to remember what is being learned. By understanding how memory works, instructional leaders can transfer that understanding to improve their own memory, their ability to be an instructional resource, their communication, and the instruction at their site. This means less time is wasted, and teachers are better able to deepen or extend their thinking, engage in learning communities, and apply their learning, which lies at the heart of improving their practice. On a personal-learning level, instructional leaders are continuously learning themselves. When one understands how memory works, one can apply that understanding to enhance encoding and later recall. This knowledge will provide a foundation for the instructional leader to recognize, identify, and analyze instruction that promotes effective recall.

Have you ever . . .

- *Landed in your driveway without a conscious memory of the drive home?*
- *Couldn't stop remembering something to your dismay?*
- *Could recall a learning experience decades after it had occurred?*

UNCONSCIOUS MEMORY

When people drive for a certain length of time (especially the exact same route), they build a level of competence and automaticity for the task, similar to how they become automatic readers of text. To do this, they use a memory system called the nondeclarative system, which is discussed in more detail later. When people perform an automatic skill, like driving home, with a great deal of repetition and success, in a similar context, their nondeclarative memory becomes quite efficient. It becomes so efficient, in fact, that the amount and need to consciously attend diminishes a little. The memory system of the driver has the route down to every bump, turn, or pothole, and it can predict exactly what eye, leg, or arm movement is needed when. This allows the driver to be thinking about things other than the task at hand. This is why people may remember what they are thinking about on the way home, but they have no recall of the act of driving (Schacter, 2001).

Things change considerably if the person suddenly sees a child's ball roll into the street or hears the skidding of tires. If something novel occurs during a drive like this, the person's consciousness arrives instantly, ready to deal with any challenges that threaten her survival. These are the drives home that people remember vividly.

REMEMBERING—EVEN
WHEN YOU DON'T WANT TO

Have you ever made a faux pas at work and suffered through the repeat performance in your head for the rest of the day (especially if the key players of the event are in your visual field)? Times when a memory is overly persistent can be as, if not more, frustrating than failing to recall a memory. The reason for these kinds of experiences is perseveration, a kind of memory hiccup that is implicated, on a grander scale, with posttraumatic stress disorder. In these instances, memory is being recalled repeatedly, to a person's detriment. Often, someone will need to begin a different task, leave the immediate location for a while, or engage in other kinds of thinking in order to put the memory to bed (Schacter, 2001).

REMEMBERING AFTER DECADES

And then there are learning experiences that are decades old that still shine in your memory, memories that have stood the test of time. For me, it was studying pioneers of the Ohio prairie in my fourth-grade social studies class. My teacher created stations where every student was given the opportunity to make, see, hear, listen, talk, and even taste (something akin to Johnny Cakes) artifacts from 1800s Ohio. The entire day was memorable, but one of the stations in particular still stands out. It was a station where students created beautiful, honey-colored candles. These were candles we would be able to take home and use on the dinner table that night. This was not only engaging; it was enjoyable, relevant, purposeful, and unique. It turns out these are a few important attributes of what makes something memorable. The teacher may or may not have realized it back then, but she designed an engaging, purposeful, episodic memory that would stay with me forever. Thank you, Mrs. Johnson.

In all of these examples, memory (or lack thereof) was at the center. So how do people remember? And are there things that can be done in schools to assist the formation and later recall of memories? Read on to discover more about the neuroscience behind memory and methods the instructional leader can look for that signal powerful memory making in classrooms.

WHAT IS MEMORY?

Memory is the vestiges of what we experience. It serves to help us hang on to information or experiences that ultimately secure our survival. In the following section, you'll explore different memory systems and learn about things we can do to create more robust, accurate memories and recall for ourselves and our students.

Memory is complex. Think about observing a lesson. A lesson includes some of the same issues involved in making a memory. A lesson can be information driven, like a social science lesson that teaches students about the importance of community, or procedure driven, like how to write capital letters. Like a lesson, a memory can be information driven or procedure driven. If a lesson is information driven, the information may take the form of explicit facts or an event. If the lesson is procedure driven, it may take the form of teaching a skill, like writing the letters of the alphabet. Lessons are limited in time and quantity of information, similar to a memory where M-space (see page 148) and working memory limit a person's ability to encode memories effectively. If too much input is attempted without enough time to process, it is like overfilling a glass with water, the puddle of information outside the glass growing, destined to be forgotten. The same is true when encoding memories. If people are taxed with too much information and not enough time to rehearse this information, they may forget more than they remember.

Timing Issues

If lessons are timed effectively and input is selected (and chunked) with care, student retention of the material and teacher efficacy can be enhanced (Sousa, 2003). Timing issues regarding memory include the fact that people have three phases of memory: short term, lasting only a few seconds; working, lasting 15 to 30 seconds; and long term, lasting an indefinite amount of time. The idea of these phases can be remembered by thinking about short-term memory as how long it might take for students to read the learning target for the day, working memory as how long it may take them to speak a sentence or ask a question regarding the topic, and long-term memory as when they answer a question on the final test of a unit. The structure in the brain that is implicated during a working memory event is the hippocampus. This structure, deep within the temporal lobes of the brain, was discussed in Chapter 1.

Another timing issue has to do with the fact that people tend to remember the most of what they learn at the beginning of a learning event, the second most at the end of the event, and the least in the late middle section of the event (Schacter, 2001; Sousa, 2003). This means that the beginning of a lesson is like gold, the end is like silver, and the middle is where the teacher becomes an alchemist, using methods to enhance memory formation. To some extent, that alchemy can be provided through rehearsal and engagement. Effective timing appears to occur in chunks of time about 10 to 20 minutes long, with some kind of short break between the next (new) content. This is valuable information for the school that uses block scheduling, where teachers have upward of 90-minute segments for their content area. A good rule of thumb for a teacher would be to break up input of content into 20-minute chunks, complete with an intro, rehearsal, and closure for each (Sousa, 2003).

The last timing issue has to do with how often and at what intervals people revisit or rehearse new information for optimum memory formation. When one of the country's foremost experts on memory was asked how often someone needs to rehearse new information for optimum recall, his answer was both simple and complex. He said that what works best is to rehearse the information you want to remember right before memory begins to fade (Cohen, 2010). Because many people can't necessarily tell when forgetting is commencing, that could be a tricky task. When pressed to clarify, he suggested a generalized time frame of rehearsing the information after a few minutes, then a few hours, then a few days, then a few months. In a classroom, that may take the form of a short period of rehearsal somewhere in the middle of the lesson, at the end of the lesson, before students leave for school, sometime the next day, next week, and next month. Perhaps assessments given to students (benchmarks, end of quarter, etc.) could be seen as a rehearsal of previously learned information. The bottom line with timing is this: Memory, like various things in the natural world, can erode over time. There are certain things that can increase or decrease this erosion. This can be valuable information for anyone dealing with helping others form robust memories. The topic of forgetting is examined in more detail later in the chapter.

An instructional leader observing instruction and processing in a classroom would want to see consistent application of rehearsal of information. This could take the form of a simple think, pair, share activity, a written or verbal summary of key concepts learned, or a drawing that depicts key learning.

Amount of Information Issue—M-Space and Chunking

If you've ever observed students grappling with information overload, you've seen the relationship between the amount of information and the ability to process it effectively. The instructional leader might see this in a fourth-grade math lesson where students are trying to complete long division. Long division requires many steps and processes. It is common to see students at this level struggling to digest so many different things at once. You might observe memory overload in a language arts lesson where the teacher is trying to have students remember the 10 pitfalls of punctuation. Either way, we are talking about an issue with M-space.

M-space is thought to be the amount (counted in units) of information people can consciously be aware of and hold in their working memory at any one time. M-space can change and increase as students develop into adults, and it can be augmented by something called chunking. Figure 6.1 shows the relationship between M-space and age.

Figure 6.1 The Development of M-Space

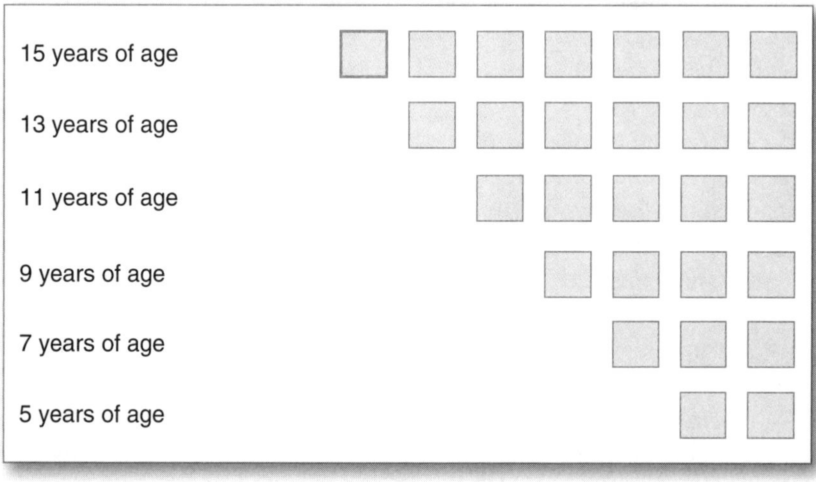

Chunking describes how people can combine bits of information to form a whole "bit," thereby conserving the amount of information to remember. It allows us to handle more bits of information (our M-space) at one time. For instance, children learn to read by learning and remembering the letters in the alphabet. After they learn their letters, they eventually begin to chunk letters into syllables, then syllables into words, words into phrases, phrases into sentences, sentences into paragraphs, and so forth. Some people have "chunked" volumes of books into their memories—a body of knowledge in their field of expertise. Because it is known that chunking facilitates remembering larger quantities of information, wise teachers could use this to their advantage when designing learning experiences for their students. Instructional leaders need to know about chunking when they observe lessons where the teacher is trying to teach too many concepts at a time or before they try to share a list of 12 new protocols with teachers at a staff meeting. Understanding why people chunk information (a) helps instructional leaders share this information with classroom teachers, (b) helps them spot it in the classroom, (c) helps them to know when to suggest using it in the classroom, and (d) helps them provide resources for teachers to embed this knowledge in their practice.

As an instructional leader, sharing information about M-space takes a minimal amount of time, but the payoff can be big. Simply sharing the visual of the M-space graphic with teachers and having them engage in a brief dialogue about it can provide a memorable resource that resonates with what teachers already know instinctively. This can be incredibly powerful. Teachers that understand M-space and chunking may plan their input with careful thought, considering how many units of information they want students to process given their ages or developmental stages. They may find ways to chunk different kinds of information for students to alleviate a crowded M-space. An example of this would be a third-grade teacher (teaches 8- and 9-year-olds) who wants students to better understand the geography of the United States. Instead of having students begin their learning by memorizing the 50 different states, they may begin with three big chunks, the West, the Midwest, and the East. This would be considerate of most third graders' M-space capacity, while at the same time showing how we can chunk many states into three basic regions. During the subsequent lessons, students would delve into more detailed parts of the geography, with a good memory of the three big pieces that are composed of several smaller pieces from which to hook their new learning. Instructional leaders would want teachers to not only be aware of the issues of timing and amount of information with regard to encoding information, but they would want to see evidence of this awareness regularly, during observations in classrooms at their site. Raising the level of awareness of this need during instruction and planning might be accomplished through staff development opportunities.

HOW DOES MEMORY WORK?

Our memories are like constellations, with a few really bright stars.

—Neal Cohen (2010)

Understanding how memory works helps the instructional leader in several ways. It serves as valuable background knowledge when creating plans for staff meetings or staff development. What has been discussed so far about how memory works will help the instructional leader determine how many pieces of information to share at any one time. How can a leader chunk categories of information to enable staff to effectively process more information in less time? What things should the instructional leader look for during the input phase of a lesson or a lesson plan the leader is examining? The following section discusses different kinds of memory and what people can do to facilitate encoding and later retrieval of information.

Although the hippocampus is an important piece of the memory-making puzzle, there is no one piece of real estate in the brain in which neuroscientists can focus their research in regard to memory. This is one of the reasons that the field of memory is so complicated. Memories live in various, elusive regions of the brain, in neural networks that mingle with different areas in the brain, areas where language, images, sounds, and movement are stored. Therefore, memories are just as unique as the neural networks of which they are a member. In fact, each time people retrieve a memory, they have to actively reconstruct that memory, searching through the various locations where bits and pieces of the memory may be stored, stitching together each new retrieval event from scratch (Squire & Kandel, 2000). This is part of the reason memory can be faulty, especially when distractions occur when encoding the memory, and why it is so vital to consider the learning environment during encoding.

DIFFERENT MEMORY SYSTEMS— DECLARATIVE AND NONDECLARATIVE

Our brains use different memory systems to remember different kinds of things (Squire & Kandel, 2000). There are two large categories of memory, declarative and nondeclarative, and they include several subcategories. There are actions we can take to enhance the encoding, storage, and retrieval of these memory systems, and they sometimes differ, depending on the nature of the content to be learned. An average day spent in school is filled with the need to flexibly store, use, and blend both kinds of memory systems, regardless of whether someone is an administrator, a teacher, or a student. The aim of the instructional leader is to observe the actions of teachers and students in classrooms to ensure that the necessary aides are in place to enhance the encoding of new memories.

Declarative Memory

Declarative memory is the kind of memory that is in charge of remembering facts, names, labels, dates, and so forth. Although declarative memories are not the only kinds of memories formed when people learn, they are a sizable chunk of what is required of students. This is the memory that remembers who the current president of the United States is, what the word diversify means, and how to spell Hawaii. Although, as mentioned earlier, there is no one structure in the brain that is solely in charge of remembering, it's important to note that there are a few "bright stars" in terms of structures that are enlisted when remembering. During the creation of declarative memories, there is evidence to suggest that aside from the hippocampus, parts of the frontal lobes are also co-opted.

DECLARATIVE MEMORIES' SUBGROUPS—SEMANTIC AND EPISODIC

Semantic Memories

There are two categories that fall under declarative memory: semantic and episodic. Semantic memories are context-free memories of knowledge, facts, ideas, and so forth: think Trivial Pursuit. These are the memories that are taxed when students take standardized tests. In order to successfully encode semantic memories, our brains need to process the information in some way. Neuroscientists have named the kind of processing that facilitates the encoding of semantic memories as rehearsal. Rehearsing information increases retention and later recall and can take various forms (Medina, 2008). Rehearsal requires the rememberer to do something, to manipulate the information somehow. Doing something with the memory might mean talking about it, writing about it, drawing an image that relates to it, or any number of similar processes. The point of rehearsal is to revisit the information. This revisiting allows the neural networks and subsequent memory to strengthen, and therefore, it is more prepared to link new information onto it. When observing teaching, the instructional leader can remember that a good time for rehearsal and elaboration (generally) is somewhere a little past the middle of the lesson. If the leader does not see some kind of rehearsal happening, it is unlikely that strong memories are being formed. In lesson plans, the instructional leader may want to have teachers determine where they will be incorporating deliberate rehearsal and elaboration of the content for students' retention of the material. In meetings where new information is expected to be learned by the staff, including rehearsal at appropriate times will increase the likelihood of later retrieval for the teachers.

Episodic Memories

Episodic memories are memories of events or episodes. These include things like assemblies, a simulation in the classroom, a debate, or a reading of a passage by the teacher. Episodic memories follow a kind of story line, and students naturally relate to story lines (Squire & Kandel, 2000). Clever teachers can use this to their advantage to create *content* story lines of sorts by attending to the stories in the content. For instance, during a science unit, teachers make overt links to what students have previously learned, like how electricity flows in a certain direction (the beginning of the story), to what they are currently learning, like how we can create circuits to control a current of electricity (the middle of the story), and how that relates to the big picture, the fact that electricity is a vital resource for human beings (the theme or title of the story; Roth, Garnier, Chen, Lemmens, Schwille, & Wickler, 2010). Instructional leaders can guide teachers to construct episodic memories when they create events around learning. They can create episodic memories that contain curricular content, much like the example discussed in a previous chapter about a fourth-grade social studies unit covering

Ohio prairie life. A pair of kindergarten teachers I know understood this principle well and exploited it effectively in their creation of a "bat cave" in their classroom every year that coincided with their unit on animals. This integrated unit was well designed and chock full of meaning and relevance. It was also interspersed with episodic, memorable events. Eating a snack in the bat cave with a friend, listening to the teacher read a science book about bats in the cave (while using a flashlight to be able to see), exploring the interesting walls of the bat cave, these events were episodes, remembered clearly by children even when lovingly recounted at their eighth-grade graduations. Episodic memory formation is a powerful factor behind field trips and why they are so valuable days or weeks later, back in the classroom. Teachers can attach new semantic memories onto rich episodes children have experienced. What makes field trips so effective for this kind of learning is that it allows the entire group of learners to experience an episode together, which provides a level playing field and allows natural revisits to the memory via nostalgia. Therefore, when deciding on funding for potential field trips, both instructional leaders and their staff should have a clear understanding about how the field trips are cogently linked to the learning targets and how they may provide a profound basis from which students can commit information to memory.

There is yet another subcategory of memory under episodic memory that is called a "flashbulb" memory. These are memories of events that include highly emotional or meaningful information. September 11th, 2001, created flashbulb memories for many people, especially those who lived in the United States at the time. Episodic memories can be robust memories, especially when they are talked about, repeated, and attended to often.

NONDECLARATIVE MEMORIES (PROCEDURAL, EMOTIONAL, AND AUTOMATIC RESPONSE)

Procedural Memories

The other big category of memory is called nondeclarative. It encompasses the subcategories of procedural, emotional, and automatic response. A procedural memory is the kind of memory used when learning a skill that requires physicality, like learning to pitch a base-ball or write the letters of one's name. Unlike a declarative memory that enlists the help of the frontal lobes, a nondeclarative memory is helped by the internal brain structure of the hippocampus. If you've ever learned how to do something physically and grew to be able to perform it without having to consciously think about it, you have experienced a procedural memory in action. A good universal exam-ple of this is learning to drive a car. The first time a person sits behind the wheel, he is busy creating semantic memories as well as proce-dural memories. He may be consciously learning information about the location of switches, or learning the icons of the instrument panel, and so forth. After a certain amount of time, rehearsal, prac-tice, and use, those once-semantic memories move into the back-ground, while procedural memories take center stage. Once a driver has his procedural memories encoded effectively, he naturally and automatically knows how and when to look for the required infor-mation that the dashboard offers. He automatically knows how to respond on a hill when in a car with a manual transmission or stick shift. No conscious thought needs to be generated in order to avoid a piece of errant tire just ahead of him in the lane on the freeway.

So what kinds of helpful procedural memories are students mak-ing at school, and how can teachers facilitate these? Think about the things that would be beneficial for students to know with automatic-ity, things that they could do without taxing their frontal lobes. A few examples might include classroom procedures, such as where homework is turned in, how to set up a science journal, or how to line up for lunch or an assembly or a fire drill. Procedural memories are encoded through practice of the skill or movement. This is why, during the first week of school, many teachers defer content for pro-cedures. They understand this type of nondeclarative memory for-mation and know that when students have procedural memories laid down, it frees them to tackle other (semantic) kinds of thinking.

Priming is a term used to describe the propensity for people to recall something that was introduced to them (earlier) in an unconscious way. For instance, as a principal, you might bring in a copy of Rodin's "The Thinker" and set it on the cabinet outside your office. The statue has "The Thinker" embossed on its base. You leave it there for a week. A month later, in a staff meeting, you have an image of "The Thinker" projecting on the wall. If you asked your staff to name this work of art, many would probably be able to, without remembering why they knew it. Some might find it more interesting than they would have without the priming. Priming can enhance learning through the triggers it can pull in our subconscious memories.

Emotional Memories

Go back to the very first memory you have from elementary school. Give yourself a moment to retrieve as much of it as you can. The memory you brought forth was probably one that contained a degree of emotion when you originally encoded it. In fact, the retrieval of the memory may elicit similar emotions now as when it was encoded, and chances are that the emotions that travel with the memory are negative (Tokuhama-Espinosa, 2011). For instance, when asked to participate in this exercise, many people will remember being in second grade and getting called upon to read aloud before they were fluent readers. The embarrassment, anger, and resentment they felt actually helped the memory stick. Emotional memories aren't always negative, but there is some evidence to suggest that a negative emotional valence adds an extra stamp of vividness to a memory, in an effort to ensure survival. Although we would never want to use negative emotions to provide that extra stamp of vividness in a classroom, teachers can take advantage of the fact that adding *positive* emotionality to a learning experience can benefit the encoding process.

Emotions can be elicited in different ways in the classroom, from a warm smile, to a story, to the excitement students feel when engaged in a game in the classroom. Understanding how emotions can foster memories can help a teacher use this information to benefit students. Things that on the surface might seem like a waste of time to an observer (like games being played and enjoyed) might be very effective for student learning and recall in the classroom. Positive simulations to teach concepts is an excellent use of emotionally charged learning. Beginning a unit in social science on the Gold Rush by having students find several hidden candy bars is a deceptively easy and enjoyable way to hook the learners and assist students in developing a context for why people acted in certain ways during that time. Instructional leaders should look for these types of activities in teachers' lesson plans. They might also consider developing professional development workshops that focus on enhancing teachers' skills in creating positive, memory-enhancing events.

Automatic Responses

Automatic response memory is why teachers should have students physically practice things like fire or earthquake drills, lockdown protocols, and so forth. Students should develop automatic responses to certain stimuli in order to be able to respond very quickly, without having to consciously think about it first. During a classroom observation, the instructional leader may see masterful teachers who have taught students an automatic response to get their attention when needed. This could be a catchphrase or word or a sound or a visual cue, like turning off the lights. This can save valuable instructional time and focus students' attention on the new task.

Everyone experiences automatic responses. When people hear a cell phone ring during an important meeting, they experience an automatic response of checking their own phone, either to see if theirs is the one disrupting the group or to turn off their own phone. In school, we are exposed to automatic response triggers like bells for the beginning of the day, the start of lunch, the end of recess, and so forth.

These memory types have been contextualized to help the instructional leader make the connections between memory formation and what goes on in schools. The following section provides information about things that help people remember, whether remembering a list of items from the grocery store or the contents of a high-stakes assessment.

SOME THINGS THAT HELP US REMEMBER

Some of the factors that influence whether we remember something include the distinctiveness of the information, the consequentiality of the information, the emotionality of the information, the amount of time the information is repeated, the meaningfulness of the information, the attentional capacity and demands of the individual trying to remember the information, and the sheer memory ability of the individual (Cohen, 2010).

Distinctiveness of the information can be manipulated. For instance, if a teacher would like a student to remember that there are three phases of matter, distinctiveness might be added if the teacher links it to a story (including images) about the time a piece of ice fell into a frying pan on the stove and went from a solid to a liquid to a gas in less than 15 seconds. That episodic event creates a distinctive memory related to how something can transform from a solid, to a liquid, and finally to a gas. Information can become increasingly distinctive when presented through multiple modalities (auditory, visual, and/or kinesthetic). This lesson incorporates strong auditory as well as visual input. The fact that it is put into a story line creates even more distinctiveness. The distinctiveness of the information to be remembered also comes into play when and if a teacher adds something novel to the input. For instance, a lesson that contains embedded formative assessments often helps to underscore the consequentiality of the information, but other methods, like playing a game where the information is an important element, using the information to solve a problem later, or learning something that is extremely relevant to one's life, will increase the consequentiality of it.

The emotionality of the learning event can be enhanced by embedding social learning structures into the lesson, like talking with other students, debating, or interviewing. Another wonderful way to enlist the help of emotionality is through simulations. Repeating the information is a pretty simple and well-known tool, but the way we have students repeat information can be made more engaging than simply regurgitating content. A teacher might have students repeat the information by creating a six-word summary or pantomime, completing a mind map, and so forth. The meaningfulness of the information trumps just about everything else. When we can't attach any meaning to content, it's like having wallpaper with no glue on the back of it. The information doesn't stick. How people remember has to do with M-space, chunking, and other developmental issues that need to be considered on a fairly individualized basis.

WHY AND HOW WE FORGET—
THE SEVEN SINS OF MEMORY

In Daniel Schacter's book, *The Seven Sins of Memory* (2001), he writes of a framework for understanding how we forget. This book illuminates seven different ways our memories fail us. These seven sins, as he has calls them, are absentmindedness, blocking, misattribution, persistence, transience, suggestibility, and finally, bias.

These seven sins refer to the things that erode memory (with the exception of persistence, which results in a perseveration of a memory). People who have forgotten where they placed their keys, forgotten it was their anniversary, or forgotten about a meeting were probably experiencing the sin of absentmindedness. This type of forgetting happens when there is a breakdown between attention and memory or lack of relevance or meaning of a memory occurs. The sin of blocking happens when people try to remember something, like the name of a specific word, and they are thwarted in their effort to retrieve it. This is also referred to as having a "tip-of-the-tongue" moment. The sin of misattribution describes when people remember something but attribute the memory to the wrong source. For instance, a principal may remember information regarding the district's new expulsion policy but attribute it to the wrong person or document, therefore potentially compromising the memory. The related sin of suggestibility occurs when memories are formed as a result of suggestions, comments, or leading questions. The sin of persistence occurs in those times as described early in this chapter, when a person would really rather not remember something, but the disturbing repetition of the memory persists. The sin of transience describes a weakening of memories over time. This sin happens naturally as time passes and other data catch people's attention and memory. If you have ever discovered that what you thought was a solid memory was completely wrong, you've probably been the recipient of bias. The sin of bias changes memories to reflect more about what we know or how we feel now than about the actual memory (Schacter, 2001).

Many of the ways our memories fail can be ameliorated by deliberate attention to making memories. In the following segment of text, a classroom vignette shows how one teacher makes the most of student memory-making capacity. The wording in italics is like having a whisper coach in the classroom, helping make overt links to the research behind memory making and how it manifests in the classroom. The elapsed time is bolded, italicized, and underlined.

SAMPLE OBSERVATION OF HOW A TEACHER EMBEDS THE PRINCIPLE

Teacher: Eighth grade

Subject and time of day: Social Science—10:00 AM

Learning target: Students will explain the conditions under which African slaves lived during passage to America.

Time observed: 20 minutes

As the principal slides into an available desk at the beginning of the social science lesson, she recognizes that students' declarative and nondeclarative memory systems are up and running. Students are reading the learning target and getting ready to make a statement regarding how that target is related to their previous work in the unit on the formation of the American colonies. *This is using the declarative system because it requires students to pull up information such as facts, dates, and understandings they have learned from movies, teacher input, readings and images from the textbook, and so forth. Concurrently, students are eliciting information from their nondeclarative memories with some of their automatic actions, such as putting their homework in the proper location, getting their social science journal from the pile on the side table, locating the learning target, and writing down their summary statement in their journal.* The teacher had primed the class for this unit of study far earlier in the year when she brought in a model of a ship similar to the ships that made their way across the Atlantic during the formation of the colonies. *This priming*

(Continued)

(Continued)

heightened interest of the topic in several students while providing some unconscious memories to surface when they finally began the unit (Squire & Kandel, 2000). After students wrote their statements in their journals, they found their learning partner and shared their thoughts before the teacher took center stage. *Students are rehearsing information through an engaging, verbal interaction.* By this point, students have tapped prior knowledge using both memory systems and made connections from their prior knowledge to what they would be learning today. *Elapsed time 3 minutes*

The teacher begins the lesson by referring to the learning target for the day and overtly linking what they will be doing today to their previous learning. *Thereby using the timing issue effectively, we tend to remember things at the beginning a little better than things in the middle of an episodic memory. She is also using the content story line method to assist the episodic memory system.* She also allows them to examine the content of an exit question she will later use as an assessment. She then asks students to randomly share what they have written in their journals. *Again, rehearsing, with the additional benefit of randomly calling—a novel structure.* After doing so, the teacher projects an image on the board that shows a beautifully drawn charcoal illustration of a black man's hands in chains. She then shares another similarly produced illustration of several black men sitting cramped together in what appears to be large sailboat. Lastly, she shows the final illustration of men filing out of a tall ship, in chains, being led onto an auctioneer's stage. She shows each illustration alone, giving students input through short lecturettes that are strung together in story. She then projects them all together. *She's using two different modalities for input, which allows for more neural networks to be tapped into, therefore facilitating more possibilities or "roads" of encoding and later retrieval. She's also, once again, taking advantage of the idea of a story line. Elapsed time 15 minutes*

The teacher then asks students to reflect on the input and write down three key points they feel are most closely tied to the big idea of the unit and why. *Again, they are rehearsing, with the extra boost of evaluation.* Students are then asked to share their responses through a short conversation with a different learning partner and respond to their partner by paraphrasing. *This is increasing the relevance and need to listen carefully, as the expectation is for students to repeat information told to them, which takes a great deal of active listening and remembering.* Next, the teacher plays a short clip from *Roots*, where the main character is speaking about the conditions under which they sailed from Africa to the mainland. *Elapsed time 18 minutes*

Afterward, the teacher randomly calls on several students to share what they learned thus far, the connections they found, and predictions about how this information and learning will lead them into the next phase of their lesson. *Again, a connection is made to content story line, as well as more rehearsal opportunities. Elapsed time 20 minutes*

WHAT ARE SOME OF THE THINGS THE TEACHER DID TO TAKE ADVANTAGE OF MEMORY SYSTEMS IN THIS EXAMPLE?

- Ensured that students were already familiar with classroom procedures so they could focus their conscious attention to their cognitive resources.

- Primed students earlier in the year by bringing in a model of an artifact from the era that they would be studying.

- Chunked the material in a way that allowed for students to digest important ideas thoroughly before moving on.

- Provided input in multiple modalities: auditory and visual.

- Sprinkled novelty judiciously throughout the lesson (use of charcoal illustrations, random calling, use of a clip from *Roots*).

- Attended to M-space throughout the lecture portion of the lesson. Students were given an appropriate amount of information to hold in mind at any one time during the lesson.

- Attended to the need for student processing at several points during the learning by stopping and having students talk or write about the topic.

- Used the content story line to help students hook new learning onto existing mental models.

- Used timing to benefit student memory making. Had students verbalize a learning target and repeat it several times during the lesson.

- Made the information relevant by making connections to what they already knew as well as making connections between what happened in the past as compared to what is happening today.

CONNECTING INSTRUCTIONAL LEADER KNOWLEDGE AND SKILL SETS TO UNDERSTANDING HOW MEMORY WORKS

Resource Provider

Using the information learned as well as the checklists and resources from the end of the chapter (see Tables 6.1–6.6), the instructional leader can begin to assist teachers in planning and instruction that elicit the formation of strong memories. Tables 6.2 to 6.4 provide information regarding different memory systems, ways to rehearse information, and a checklist for robust memories. These will serve as resources to guide some teachers in their learning and challenge others to advance their already proficient understanding.

Instructional Resource

The instructional leader who understands how memory works, as well as what strategies and methods enhance encoding and later retrieval, can act as a dynamic instructional resource for teachers. The rubric in Table 6.1 will assist the instructional leader in measuring teacher understanding as well as progress with regard to teaching in a way that students remember. Having the knowledge and skills to observe effectiveness of teaching and learning with regard to robust memories and later communicating that information with teachers can lead to critical improvement in teaching and learning, as well as motivation and collegiality. Sharing information about how memory works through brief presentations at staff meetings, sanctioned staff development, or modeling in classrooms would be an additional way the instructional leader could act as an instructional resource.

Understanding and applying how memory works will help the instructional leader when examining lesson plans or helping a teacher design a memorable learning experience. Table 6.5 compares effective and ineffective rehearsal strategies used in the classroom. Using resources such as these will allow the instructional leader to compare the contents of a lesson plan with known effective practices. If an instructional leader notices that no time is afforded for rehearsal of the information, a common flaw in lesson plans, she can help guide the teacher in revision of the lesson with a firm grasp on the rationale behind it. Or when a lesson plan proves to be irrelevant to students, the instructional leader can assist the teacher in amending the lesson to add relevance for increased recall.

The instructional leader can use the resources provided before, during, and after a classroom observation to become comfortable with recognizing and labeling the components of instruction that help form robust memories. This will allow the instructional leader to provide effective, specific feedback to teachers regarding this critical component of learning.

Good Communicator

These chapters have discussed the different stages of memory (short term, working, and long term), space limitations with regard to M-space, and factors that enhance memories. By applying this information in communication, an instructional leader can increase effectiveness by doing things such as chunking material, avoiding communication overload, embedding distinctiveness to the information, or ensuring some kind of rehearsal of the material through conversation. This kind of effective communication enhances vital interpersonal skills as well.

CHAPTER SUMMARY

In order to understand and learn, we must remember. Memory is a complex principle partly because there is no single structure in the brain that contains it. There are different kinds of memory. The two big categories are declarative (facts, names, dates,) and nondeclarative (skills, procedures, and unconscious memory). These different kinds of memory can be enhanced by repeating and "doing something" with the information or skill. This is called rehearsal.

Timing issues included in memory formation have to do with short-term, working, and long-term memory; determining optimal intervals for rehearsal; and attending to prime time and downtime. Space issues consider M-space, a developmental phenomenon that allows people to hold a certain number of units in the conscious working memory at any one time.

The formation of memories includes factors such as the distinctiveness, consequentiality, emotionality, repetition, meaningfulness, attentional capacity of the learner, and the sheer memory ability of the learner. These factors can be manipulated in a classroom to transform the unmemorable to the unforgettable. The factors that contribute to why we forget include absentmindedness, transience, blocking, misattribution, bias, suggestibility, and persistence.

POSTASSESSMENT CHAPTER 6—MEMORY

1. I understand the difference between declarative and nondeclarative memory systems.

2. I understand the three different phases of memory (short term, working, and long term).

3. I can describe some things that inhibit robust memory formation in a classroom.

4. I can describe some strategies that enhance memory in a classroom.

5. I can evaluate a lesson in terms of attention to memory.

QUESTIONS FOR STUDY GROUP

1. How has your understanding of how memory works changed after reading this chapter?

2. What do you feel is the most critical information from this chapter to share with teachers or other adults at your school or district?

3. What might you do differently in response to reading this chapter?

Table 6.1 Rubric for Principals—Measuring the Principles of Memory in the Classroom

Criteria	Beginning	Developing	Practicing	Exemplifying
Understanding the content topic of memory **Knowledge, comprehension**	Teacher does not yet know or understand the tenets of memory.	Teacher is just starting his learning about memory systems and cannot yet indicate differences among them.	Teacher has an understanding of the two big categories of memories (declarative and nondeclarative).	Teacher has a thorough understanding of the two big categories of memories as well as the subcategories therein.
Relating ideas from the topic to the classroom and applying them **Analysis, application**	Teacher cannot relate ideas or actions from her practice to ideas regarding memory.	Teacher can relate one idea she has learned about memory to her practice and apply it.	Teacher takes ideas about M-space and chunking and uses it at times to design effective lessons.	Teacher takes many ideas from memory formation and consistently applies them in lessons, resulting in higher student recall.
Determining which methods and strategies will best enhance memory making in situations **Application, synthesis, evaluation**	Teacher does not yet apply the methods that help increase retrieval of information.	Teacher experiments with having students rehearse information of new content in some way.	Teacher regularly embeds some kind of rehearsal strategy in lessons and can provide rationale for its sequence in the lesson.	Teacher consistently and deliberately embeds effective rehearsal and other memory-enhancing strategies during delivery of new content as well as established content.

This rubric can be used as a beginning assessment to gauge understanding, as well as to measure teachers' growth in knowledge and application of the principles of memory in their practice.

Table 6.2   Ways to Rehearse Information for the Classroom Teacher

☐ Write down the key idea(s).

☐ Write a headline for the information.

☐ Write a six-word summary.

☐ Write a limerick, haiku, or couplet.

☐ Write about the connections you make.

☐ Write about how you will use this learning.

☐ Write about how this learning has changed your previous mental model.

☐ Write about how this learning links to past learning.

☐ Talk to another student using any of the aforementioned structures.

☐ Predict how this learning will relate to future learning.

☐ Make an analogy for this learning.

☐ Craft a multiple choice question regarding this topic.

☐ Craft an essay question regarding this topic.

☐ Craft a cloze sentence or paragraph using this topic.

☐ Complete a mind map, Thinking Map, or other visual tool.

☐ Draw an icon that represents the idea(s).

☐ Draw a cartoon that represents the idea(s).

☐ Draw a picture with a caption about the idea(s).

☐ Come up with a movement that captures the idea(s) of the learning.

☐ Figure out how this idea is similar to another idea.

☐ Think about how this idea is different from another idea.

☐ Come up with a song for this learning.

☐ Create a case study that uses this learning.

☐ Brainstorm as many things in one minute that you can remember from the lesson.

Table 6.3 Memory Systems in the Real World

Memory System	Definition	This is used when . . .	Encoding Strategies	Classroom Example
Explicit/Declarative				
Episodic	An episodic memory is a memory that involves an episode, or event of some kind.	An event has taken place that a person is able to retrieve (the times, places, sequence) with relative ease, like an outing or having breakfast.	Episodic memories are made through events inside and outside of the classroom. They are retrieved with relative ease, especially when triggering cues such as a reminder of the event is presented. This could come in the form of a sound, a smell, an image, or a movement.	Teacher and students collect information and artifacts for a unit of study about Native Americans from the colonial era. They invite other classrooms or groups of students to view the collection and then the students teach the visitors about Native American customs and historical relevance.
Semantic	Semantic memories are memories of static facts and figures.	A person stores and retrieves facts and information required—the what of learning.	Elaborative rehearsal strategies help store and eventually retrieve semantic memories. These include such structures as social learning (think, pair, share activities; peer teaching, etc.), summarizing learning, use of Thinking Maps or other visual tools, and a generation of questions about the topic.	Students are given the opportunity to create their own mind map or graphic organizer regarding how negative numbers are used in the real world and then share this information with a peer.

(Continued)

Table 6.3 (Continued)

Memory System	Definition	This is used when . . .	Encoding Strategies	Classroom Example
Implicit/Nondeclarative				
Procedural	A procedural memory is a memory that involves a procedure or physical skill.	A person uses this memory system when a procedure, skill, or movement is learned—the how of learning.	Encoding strategies that help store and retrieve procedural memories are repetition of the procedure or skill, deliberate at first, then eventually becoming unconscious.	Students prepare their paper for an assignment and place it in the correct location in the classroom when the assignment has been completed.
Conditioned response	A conditioned response is a memory that is automatically retrieved.	People might use this system when hearing a certain sound they know to indicate an immediate action will follow.	Encoding strategies that store conditioned response memories can happen at an automatic, unconscious level, but repetition is required.	The fire alarm rings and students automatically file out of the classroom silently and know exactly where to go on the blacktop.
Emotional	A memory that co-opts the amygdala due to the emotional valence of the event.	A person might encode or retrieve an emotional memory when experiencing something that evokes an emotional response.	Encoding strategies that encourage emotional memories include methods such as storytelling, simulations, personal response, social learning, and novelty.	Students participate in a simulation that elicits the same kinds of emotional responses that the content they are learning (e.g., the first Thanksgiving) may have elicited when it occurred in reality.

Table 6.4 Teachers' Checklist for Robust Memory Makers

☐ I craft lessons that are grounded in meaningful, relevant information.

☐ I make visible in my classroom what students are expected to learn.

☐ I verbalize what students are going to learn, what I'm going to teach.

☐ I occasionally have my students announce what they are going to learn.

☐ I use multiple modalities for input and output of information.

☐ I deliberately choose processing strategies that elicit the thinking or procedures necessary for success.

☐ When teaching procedures, students always repeat them physically.

☐ When teaching declarative information, I have students make sense of information.

☐ Student frequently repeat information to others during a lesson.

☐ I regularly use exit cards as a memory trigger.

☐ I chunk the material and attend to M-space when designing or executing lessons.

☐ There is a consequence to remembering in my classroom.

☐ I carefully consider timing when developing a lesson.

☐ I deliberately plan a closure activity for students.

☐ I make information distinctive in some way.

☐ I create (or have students create) associations to enhance memory of content.

☐ I link the content storyline to the lesson.

☐ I frequently check for understanding to catch misconceptions in the making.

☐ I remind students of past learning and how it links to the current learning.

☐ I use strategies like mnemonics when appropriate.

☐ I use emotions to enhance lessons.

☐ I have students summarize what they have learned.

☐ I use priming when appropriate and helpful.

☐ I put things into rhythm, rhyme, or music if possible.

☐ I use what the students are interested in as a vehicle to hook new learning.

☐ I have students show what they remember in multiple modalities.

☐ I use images and color with students to help encode and retrieve memories

Table 6.5 Effective and Ineffective Strategies the Instructional Leader May See in a Classroom

Issue at Hand	Ineffective Strategies	Instead . . .
M-space issue, timing issue	Students are asked to listen or watch input for more than 15 minutes at a time without any rehearsal strategies embedded.	Teacher chunks material in brief episodes which are followed by rehearsal times at regular intervals.
Nondeclarative (procedural) issue	Students don't get a chance to internalize different routines in the classroom, as evidenced by aimless wandering.	Students are so familiar with classroom routines that they can independently perform routine tasks on a consistent basis.
Input (planning for relevance) issue	Material presented to students lacks any kind of relevance to the students' world or life experiences.	Teacher deliberately plans lessons/units that include the relevance to students and purpose for the learning.
Input (planning for emotional hook) issue	Delivery is lacking in any kind of emotional response.	Emotional hooks are used to increase attention, engagement, and interest as well as understanding and retention of the material.
Content storyline issue	There are no overt linkages made from the current learning to the past or future learning by teacher or students.	Teacher deliberately and overtly links past learning to current and future learning.
Episodic or emotional memory issue	Teacher makes no effort to create learning events that include episodes for students to later recall (simulations, debates, etc.).	Teacher includes strategy simulations, debates, field trips, and role-play activities in their instruction.
Input and M-space issues, short-term memory issues	The environment in the classroom during learning experiences includes numerous distractions that disrupt memory formation.	Students understand and observe quiet times in class, especially during a processing event.
M-space issue	Students are asked to remember 15 rules for punctuation in one lesson.	Teacher refers to M-space within the students' developmental level. Students are not asked to remember more units than is reasonably possible.

Issue at Hand	Ineffective Strategies	Instead . . .
M-space issue Timing issue Rehearsal issue	The entire lesson consists of lecture.	If lecture is the primary mode of input, the teacher embeds processing activities during the lecture, such as open-ended questions, think, pair, share activities, etc.
Limited retrieval issue	The entire lesson consists of one modality—entirely auditory, visual, or kinesthetic.	The lesson's input includes more than one modality—auditory coupled with visual, visual coupled with kinesthetic, etc.
Rehearsal issue	The teacher calls on one student who has voluntarily raised his hand to answer a key concept and assumes the whole class will remember what was said.	The teacher uses random methods to call on students or has student process verbally with a partner before calling on anyone.
Rehearsal issue	Assumption is made that if the class chorally responds to a key question correctly, all students will remember it.	The teacher includes key question in an exit card or brief assessment at the end of the class period for individual completion.
Content storyline issue, rehearsal issue	The closure to the lesson is ambiguous or absent.	The closure includes a brief review of the key learning for the day, how it relates to the big ideas of the unit, and how it will be related to future learning.
Nondeclarative issue	Assumption is made that if students see an example, they will remember how to do something.	Students actually perform the psychomotor task requested by the teacher.
Rehearsal issue	The teacher does not leave (enough) time for processing after input has been given.	Teacher ensures that enough processing time will be available, even if it means eliminating the least important concept in a lesson.
Closure issue	Assumption is made that if students are engaged in a task, they will remember it later.	Teacher consistently asks students to prove what they remember through verbal, written, or kinesthetic tasks.

Table 6.6   Additional Resources to Find Out More About Memory

Books:

How To Teach So Students Remember—Marilee Sprenger (2005)

Learning and Memory: The Brain In Action—Marilee Sprenger (1999)

Memory: From Mind to Molecules—Larry Squire and Eric Kandel (2000)

The Seven Sins of Memory—Daniel Schacter (2001)

Searching for Memory—Daniel Schacter (1996)

Your Memory: A User's Guide—Alan Baddeley (2004)

Websites for Adults:

http://www.brainconnection.com

http://www.mindmatters.com

http://www.exploratorium.edu/memory/

http://www.youramazingbrain.org/yourmemory

http://www.newhorizons.org/strategies/arts/brewer.htm

http://www.cdl.org/resource-library/articles/memory_pt3.php

Websites for Students:

http://www.zefrank.com/memory

http://www.exploratorium.edu/memory

http://www.coolmath-games.com/memory

http://www.word-buff.com

Resources for Student Memory:

Computer accessible memory games

Old-fashioned memory games

Brain Safari software

Endnote

My hope is that this book has provided the instructional leader with information, inspiration, ideas, and food for thought. As a final note, there are few big ideas that are worth reiterating and putting into the context of our charge as educators, instructional leaders, teachers, and even parents.

THE INSTRUCTIONAL LEADER AS A GAME CHANGER

Instructional leaders who understand how we learn can have a tremendous positive impact on their entire school on various levels. Improvements in students' academic achievement, social-emotional environments, morale and engagement of students and staff, and communication and efficacy can be the by-products of the instructional leader who is equipped and confident regarding how they learn.

THE OPTIMISM OF THE PLASTIC BRAIN

Science has given us a solid foundation from which to be optimistic about the ability of the human brain to sculpt, change, and rewire itself through different experiences. These experiences can make us smarter, healthier, more engaged human beings. Plasticity makes it possible for the mediocre teacher to become the great teacher, for the principal who has trouble with public speaking to develop into a masterful communicator, and maybe, most importantly, for the child who sees school as a series of disappointments to see, instead, his own success.

EMOTIONS ARE CRITICAL FOR LEARNING

Just about every decision people make is based, somewhat, on emotions. And although science provides us with copious amounts of information, facts, and anecdotes on how emotions impact learning, this is perhaps most deeply understood through one's own experience. Just about everyone has experienced a negative emotional event that left them speechless or frozen in fear. Our emotions and the emotions of our students do not stop at the classroom door or schoolyard gate. Understanding the repercussions of positive and negative emotions on a learner is a critical message for not only the instructional leader, but for teachers, students and parents as well.

ENGAGEMENT = LEARNING

The kinds of skills our children need to be successful contributing members of society look different now than they did in the past. Twenty-first-century skills include habits of mind and ways of thinking that require engagement. Skills like problem solving, collaborating, working in a team, and being flexible and adaptable, curious and empathic, are just a few that the students of the future need to be able to flourish. These are not necessarily easy to teach or assess, but they are vital nonetheless. Understanding some of the tenets of what the brain finds worthy of attending to and engaging in is an avenue to these skills. Where there is true engagement, there is true learning.

THE POWER OF PROCESSING

The field of neuroscience has delivered news in the past decade that unveils some of the mystery of the black box in our heads. With that news have come insights about what kinds of mental moves people make to process information as well as how they might enhance the processing of certain kinds of information. Teaching anyone, regardless of age, without allowing for time and ways to process, would be like walking through the Louvre without taking your eyes off of your Blackberry. Processing effectively can move a person from compliance to critical thinking.

FEEDBACK HELPS EVERYONE

Feedback can motivate, teach, clarify, and provide a rich context from which to reflect. Whether we are talking about an instructional leader giving written feedback to a teacher regarding a strategy she witnessed, a teacher providing verbal feedback about his students' accents in a language class, or a coach giving feedback in the form of a demonstration to the track and field team, good feedback is one of the most effective ways to improve any kind of practice. Understanding how feedback assists a learner, the different types of feedback, and the various ways to deliver it can help the instructional leader help anyone learn.

REMEMBERING = KNOWING

To remember is to know. And every educator (not to mention every student) is required to know a whole lot these days. It was once thought that the capacity to remember was static, but along with plasticity, science has brought forth information regarding the possibility for improving and enhancing a person's ability to remember. This is very good news for instructional leaders, teachers, and students. Having a grasp of how memory is encoded and recalled results in the kind of understanding that allows educators to teach in ways that result in robust memories.

THE GIFTS OF SCIENCE ENHANCE
THE ART OF TEACHING

In the past decade, the field of education has been challenged by an onslaught of issues. But the good news is, the field of neuroscience has given us new tools to resolve many of these issues. We have been forced to examine our practices as educators and thoroughly analyze the ways in which we work in education. Out of this evaluation have come innovations and a desire for improvement from all stakeholders. These innovations take the forms of things like professional learning communities, educational rounds, the growth of STEM (Science, Technology, Engineering, and Math) schools and International Baccalaureate programs, and so forth.

The skills and habits of mind we will need for the 21st century are embedded in these practices and programs.

I believe the field of neuroscience has given all educators a great gift in the past decade. With the advent of technologies that allow us to see inside our heads, and the help of some wonderful translators in both areas of science and education, we are stitching together powerful foundational understanding regarding learning and teaching. How we optimally learn is becoming less and less mysterious with each passing day, and because of that, the art of teaching is becoming more and more accessible. Understanding this gift that we have been given can change the face of our educational system. I believe it is incumbent upon educators to not only recognize this gift, but unwrap it, use it, and share it with others.

References

Antonetti, J. (2007). *Writing as a measure and model of thinking.* Phoenix, AZ: Colleagues on Call.

Armstrong, T. (2010). *Neurodiversity: Discovering the extraordinary gifts of autism, ADHD, dyslexia, and other brain differences.* Cambridge, MA: Da Capo Lifelong.

Baddeley, A. (2004). *Your memory: A user's guide.* Buffalo, NY: Firefly Books.

Bolte-Taylor, J. (2006). *My stroke of insight.* New York, NY: Penguin.

Brafman, O. (2008). *The irresistible pull of irrational behavior.* New York, NY: Doubleday.

Brookhart, S. (2008). *How to give effective feedback to your students.* Alexandria, VA: Association for Supervision and Curriculum Development.

Brookover, W. B, & Lezotte, L. (1982). *Creating effective schools.* Holmes Beach, FL: Learning Publication.

BTSA. (2010, October). Beginning Teacher Support and Assessment Training, Ontario-Montclair School District.

Caine, N., Caine, G., McClintic, C., & Klimek, K. (2009). *12 brain/mind learning principles in action: Developing executive functions of the human brain.* Thousand Oaks, CA: Corwin.

Caine, R., & Caine, G. (1991). *Making connections: Teaching and the human brain.* Menlo Park, CA: Addison-Wesley Publishing Company.

Carter, R. (2009). *The human brain book.* London: DK Pub.

Cohen, N. (2010, January). *Memory . . . systems of the brain . . . and amnesia . . . in the media . . . and the law.* Paper presented at the Brain Renewal Conference—Memory, Napa, CA.

Costa, A., & Garmston, R. (2002). *Cognitive coaching: A foundation for renaissance schools.* Norwood, MA: Christopher-Gordon.

Csikszentmihalyi, M. (1990). *Flow: The psychology of optimal experience.* New York, NY: Harper Perennial.

Daggett, W. (2008). *Rigor and relevance from concept to reality.* Rexford, NY: International Center for Leadership in Education.

Damasio, A. (1994). *Descartes' error.* New York, NY: Penguin.

Damasio, A. (2003). *Looking for Spinoza: Joy, sorrow, and the feeling brain.* Orlando, FL: Harcourt Brace.

Danielson, C. (2007). *Enhancing professional practice: A framework for teaching.* Alexandria, VA: Association for Supervision and Curriculum Development.

Denton, P. (2007). *The power of our words: Teacher language that helps children learn.* Turners Falls, MA: Northeast Foundation for Children.

DePorter, B., Reardon, M., & Singer-Nourie, S. (1999). *Quantum teaching: Orchestrating student success.* Boston, MA: Allyn & Bacon.

Diamond, A. (2009, November 19). "Learning, Doing, Being—A New Science of Education" (NPR interview). Retrieved from http://speaking offaith.publicradio.org/programs/2009/learning-doing-being/.

DuFour, R., Eaker, R., & DuFour, R. (2005). *On common ground: The power of professional learning communities.* Bloomington, IN: National Educational Service.

Dweck, C. (2006). *Mindset: The new psychology of success.* New York, NY: Ballantine.

Ekman, P. (2003). *Emotions revealed: Recognizing faces and feelings to improve communication and emotional life.* New York, NY: Owl.

Elmore, R., City, A., Fiarman, S., & Teitel, L. (2009). *Instructional rounds in education: A network approach to improving teaching and learning.* Cambridge, MA: Harvard Education.

Fullan, M. (1991). *The new meaning of educational change.* New York, NY: Teachers College Press.

Garmston, R., & Wellman, B. (2009). *The adaptive school: A sourcebook for developing collaborative groups.* Norwood, MA: Christopher-Gordon.

Glenn, S. (1990) *Positive discipline in the classroom.* New York, NY: Random House.

Hart, L. (1983). *Human brain and human learning.* White Plains, NY: Longman.

Haslam, S. A., & Knight, C. (2010). *Cubicle sweet cubicle: The best ways to make office spaces not so bad.* Retrieved from http://www.scientificamerican.com/article.cfm?id=cubicle-sweet-cubicle.

Hattie, J. (2009). *Visible Learning: A Synthesis of over 800 Meta-Analyses Relating to Achievement.* New York, NY: Routledge.

Hyerle, D. (2000). *A field guide to using visual tools.* Alexandria, VA: Association for Supervision and Curriculum Development.

Hyerle, D. (2009). *Visual tools for transforming information into knowledge.* Thousand Oaks, CA: Corwin.

James, W. (1890). *Principles of psychology.* Cambridge, MA: Harvard University Press.

Jensen, E. (2006). *Enriching the brain: How to maximize every learner's potential.* San Francisco, CA: Jossey-Bass.

Jones, F. (2007). *Fred Jones tools for teaching* (2nd ed.). Santa Cruz, CA: Author.

Kagan, S. (1994). *Cooperative learning.* San Clemente, CA: Kagan Publishing.

Lambert, K. (2008, July). *Depressingly easy.* Retrieved from http://www .scientificamerican.com/article.cfm?id=depressingly-easy.

LeDoux, J. (1996). *The emotional brain: The mysterious underpinnings of emotional life.* New York, NY: Simon & Schuster.

LeDoux, J. (2002) *Synaptic Self.* New York, NY. Penguin Books.

Madison, L. (2002). *The feelings book: The care and keeping of your emotions.* Middleton, WI: Pleasant Company Publications.

Marshall, K. (2009). *Rethinking teacher supervision and evaluation: How to work smart, build collaboration, and close the achievement gap.* San Francisco, CA: Jossey-Bass.

Martin, A., & Downson, M. (2009). Interpersonal relationships, motivation, engagement and achievement: Yields for theory, current issues, and educational practice. *Review of Educational Research, 79*(1), 327–365.

Marzano, J. (2003). *What works in schools: Translating research into action.* Alexandria, VA: Association for Supervision and Curriculum Development.

Marzano, J. (2007). *The art and science of teaching: A comprehensive framework for effective instruction.* Alexandria, VA: Association for Supervision and Curriculum Development.

Medina, J. (2008). *Brain rules: 12 principles for surviving and thriving at work, home, and school.* Seattle, WA: Pear.

Medina, J. (2009, February). *Brain rules.* Paper presented at the conference of the Learning and Brain Society, San Francisco, CA.

Moore, B. (2009). Emotional intelligence for school administrators: A priority for school reform. *American Secondary Education, 37*(3), 20–28.

Morris, R. (1995). *Tools and toys.* San Diego, CA: New Management.

Morris, R. (1997). *New management.* San Diego, CA: New Management.

National Research Council. (1999). *How people learn: Brain, mind experience and school.* Washington, DC: National Academy Press.

National Urban Alliance. (2009). National Urban Alliance Training.

Nelson, J., Lott, L., & Glenn, S. H. (2000). *Positive discipline in the classroom.* New York, NY: Random House.

Noddings, N. (1988). Schools face crisis in caring. *Education Week, 8*(14), 32.

Pert, C. (1997). *Molecules of emotion: Why you feel the way you feel.* New York, NY: Touchstone.

Phillips, J. (2002). *Manager-Administrator to instructional leader: Shift in the role of the school principal.* Retrieved from http://peoplelearn .homestead.com/PrincipaInstructLeader.htm.

Popham, J. (2008). *Transformative assessment.* Alexandria, VA: Association for Supervision and Curriculum Development.

Ratey, J. (2001). *A user's guide to the brain.* New York, NY: Pantheon.

Ratey, J. (2008, September 5). *John Ratey MD discusses ADD* (Brain Science Podcast #45). Retrieved from http://www.brainsciencepodcast.com/bsp/john-ratey-md-discusses-add-bsp-45.html.

Ratey, J., & Hagerman, E. (2008). *Spark: The revolutionary new science of exercise and the brain.* New York, NY: Little, Brown.

Reeves, D. (2006). *The learning leader: How to focus school improvement for better results.* Alexandria, VA: Association for Supervision and Curriculum Development.

Roam, D. (2008). *The back of the napkin: Solving problems and selling ideas with pictures.* New York, NY: Portfolio.

Roth, K., Garnier, H., Chen, C., Lemmens, M., Schwille, K., & Wickler, N. (2010). Videobased lesson analysis: Effective science PD for teacher and student learning. *Journal of Research in Science Teaching, 48*(2), 117–148.

Rotner, S. (2003). *Lots of feelings.* Minneapolis, MN: Millbrook Press.

Sapolsky, R. (2004). *Why zebras don't get ulcers.* New York, NY: Henry Holt.

Schacter, D. (1996). *Searching for memory.* New York, NY: Basic Books.

Schacter, D. (2001). *The seven sins of memory: How the mind forgets and remembers.* Boston, MA: Houghton Mifflin.

Schlechty, P. (2002). *Working on the work: An action plan for teachers, principals, and superintendents.* San Francisco, CA: Jossey-Bass.

Sousa, D. (2003). *The leadership brain: How to lead today's schools more effectively.* Thousand Oaks, CA: Corwin.

Sousa, D. (2006). *How the brain learns.* Thousand Oaks, CA: Corwin.

Sousa, D. (2009). *How the brain influences behavior: Management strategies for every classroom.* Thousand Oaks, CA: Corwin.

Sousa, D. (2010). *Mind, brain and education: Implications for the educator.* Bloomington, IN: Solution Tree.

Spelman, C. (2000). *When I feel angry.* Morton Grove, IL: Albert Whitman & Company.

Spelman, C. (2002a). *When I feel sad.* Morton Grove, IL: Albert Whitman & Company.

Spelman, C. (2002b). *When I feel scared.* Morton Grove, IL: Albert Whitman & Company.

Sprenger, M. (1999). *Learning and Memory: The brain in action.* Alexandria, VA: Association for Curriculum and Development.

Sprenger, M. (2005). *How to teach so students remember.* Alexandria, VA: Association for Supervision and Curriculum Development.

Squire, L., & Kandel, E. (2000). *Memory: From mind to molecules.* New York, NY: Scientific American Library.

Standing, L. (1973) Learning in 10,000 pictures. *Quarterly Journal of Experimental Psychology, 25,* 207–222.

Stiggins, R., Arter, J., Chappuis, J., & Chappuis, S. (2004). *Classroom assessment for student learning: Doing it right, using it well.* Portland, OR: Assessment Training Institute.

Stronge, J., Tucker, P., & Hindman, J. (2004). *Handbook for qualities of effective teachers.* Alexandria, VA: Association for Supervision and Curriculum Development.

Tokuhama-Espinosa, T. (2011). *Mind, brain, and education science: A comprehensive guide to the new brain-based teaching.* New York, NY: W. W. Norton.

VanDeWeghe, R. (2009). *Engaged learning.* Thousand Oaks, CA: Corwin.

Vygotsky, L. (1978). *Mind in society: The development of higher psychological processes.* Cambridge, MA: Harvard University Press.

Whitaker, B. (1997). Instructional leadership and principal visibility. *The Clearing House: A Journal of Educational Strategies, Issues and Ideas, 70*(3), 155–156.

Willingham, D. (2009). *Why don't students like school?: A cognitive scientist answers questions about how the mind works and what it means for the classroom.* San Francisco, CA: Jossey-Bass.

Willis, J. (2010). *How your child learns best.* Naperville, IL: Sourcebooks.

Wolfe, P. (2010). *Brain matters: Translating research into classroom practice.* Alexandria, VA: Association for Supervision and Curriculum Development.

Zull, J. (2002). *The art of changing the brain: Enriching teaching by exploring the biology of learning.* Sterling, VA: Stylus.

Index

CORWIN
A SAGE Company

The Corwin logo—a raven striding across an open book—represents the union of courage and learning. Corwin is committed to improving education for all learners by publishing books and other professional development resources for those serving the field of PreK–12 education. By providing practical, hands-on materials, Corwin continues to carry out the promise of its motto: **"Helping Educators Do Their Work Better."**